Songs from an Armchair

Quicksilver Publications

Songs from an Armchair

a book in praise of old age

Stephanie Smith
and the members of the
Wisma Mulia Poetry Group

First published by Quicksilver Publications in the United Kingdom in 2012

Copyright © Stephanie Smith
This edition published 2012

ISBN 978-0-9571875-0-4

All rights reserved. No part of this publication may be reproduced, stored in a retrieval system, or transmitted, in any form, or by any means, electronic, mechanical, photocopying, recording or otherwise, without the prior permission of the publisher and copyright holder.

Stephanie Smith has asserted the moral right to be identified as the author of this work.

www.songsfromanarmchair.co.uk

Typeset in Jazz and Hoeffler 12 point plus others
Origination by Quicksilver Publications
Printed and bound by Berforts Group Ltd., Stevenage, Herts

This book is dedicated to all who fear the onset of old age, either for themselves or for their loved ones.

How beautifully the leaves grow old. How full of light and colour are their last days.
John Burroughs

Contents

Chapter 1	The Beginning	1
Chapter 2	Test Run	8
Chapter 3	Settling In	15
Chapter 4	In Concert	19
Chapter 5	Our Book	27
Chapter 6	The Poems	33
Chapter 7	Interviews with the Group Members	115
Chapter 8	About Wisma Mulia	189

Illustrations

Front cover image by Philip Skinner and Bryony Critchley
Liberty bodice photo by kind permission of Leicestershire
    County Council Museum Service   page 82
Rose window, Chartres Cathedral, France, John Gibson-Forty
                                    pages 100, 101
Ladies of the group by Patrick Callaghan, Stephanie Smith
    and Trish Mills
Wisma Mulia photos by Josh James
Colour photos of Wisma Mulia Garden Party by
    Stephanie Smith
Original line drawings by Maryse Lawrie   57, 67, 74
Original paintings of mandalas by Hosanna
                            colour plate section, 99, 187
Miscellaneous drawings taken from beloved books
    long out of copyright, including Royal Princess Readers
    Book 5, 1901; East of the Sun and West of the Moon, 1932;
    The British Bird Book, 1930.

Foreword

When the Chairman of the Board of Wisma Mulia, David Barker, told me of a chance encounter with a certain Stephanie Smith, he suggested I should speak to her about joining our team of volunteers. He described her as 'a volunteer with talent' who might be able to add some *je ne sais quoi* to our already vibrant and creative community.

This lady with a commanding and engaging presence walked into my office and I immediately knew that we were about to embark on an exciting and interesting journey. She told me that she felt the residents needed poetry. My initial thought was Why?, quickly followed by 'You don't know our residents!'

My first words, however, were, 'That would be lovely,' and 'Good luck with that.'

Those who live at Wisma Mulia know exactly what they want, and I wondered how she would convince them of their 'need' for poetry. What I didn't see at that first meeting was the vision and determination of this impressive lady to persevere. And persevere she did!

I didn't sit in on those early sessions in the sitting room where Steph skilfully extracted the hidden passions, hurts and fun of our wonderful team of poets. I didn't see the tears of frustration either in the early weeks when our courageous volunteer battled with doubt as to whether it would 'work'. Neither did I see those first moments when beauty and words combined to bring a re-emergence of the depth of feelings and experience that only age can bring.

The full extent of how wrong I had been to doubt this lady was evident at one of our regular concerts for family and friends when the team of poets graced us for the first time with their moving and insightful literary creations.

I am still not entirely sure how she succeeded but there is no doubt that she did, and the enduring legacy of her work and relationship with our residents continues to have an impact on our community.

This gem of a book reminds us that poetry has the power to reveal the richness of the soul and allow our humanity and spirituality to combine and flourish – whatever our age.

Philip James
Manager

Acknowledgements

First, thanks must go to Dimitri Waring for pointing the way to Wisma Mulia and a great adventure. None of this would have happened without him.

To Philip James for having unquestioning faith in me.

To Mary Thomas, for support and encouragement when I wanted to give up.

To Dawn Ives, for her invaluable and always prompt assistance in constructing a book from a distance.

To all the staff members who contributed in a hundred ways to keeping our group alive and vibrant.

To Monica Jones, for giving up her time, skill and energy to fill in the gaps.

To Esther McLaughlin at Sweet Potato Designs, for conjuring up our website with such skill and enthusiasm.

To my family, and especially my partner, for going on listening.

And finally, this book would not be what it is without the skill, passion and consummate professionalism of my friend, editor and publisher, Trish Mills, who gives it everything she's got and seems never to sleep.

Chapter 1

The Beginning

It was 2010. I was sixty four years old and had been trying for a year to find some voluntary work that suited my experience, interests and availability. I had been increasingly bemused at just how difficult that was proving to be. Having originally trained as an actress and teacher of drama, my working life had encompassed teaching, training, Speech and Language Therapy, counselling, management of a residential drug and alcohol facility and, for the last seven years, running a small B&B in the middle of a vineyard in southwest France.

Now I was back in England having a new adventure, living with my partner and our ginger cat, Oscar, on a beautiful 70 ft narrowboat in Gloucestershire. Life was good and I was enjoying having time to write short stories and make a stab at a novel for the first time in my life. I could spare a day a week to be useful to someone.

One of the obstacles to taking even a voluntary post was the fact that, since my retirement, we regularly spent only nine months of any year in England. Winters – January to April – were spent with my partner's daughter, who lives in Thailand. And it was on a small island in the southern Gulf of Thailand that I got into conversation with Dimitri Waring. Dimitri and his wife Natalie ran Ink Book Store, which offered a convivial setting for a small writers' group that I belonged to. Dimitri had not lived in England for more than fifteen years.

"So, you have a narrowboat," he commented. "Where do you moor it?"

"Oh, nowhere you would have heard of. It's close to a tiny village in Gloucestershire called Frampton-on-Severn."

"Frampton? Really? I know it well."

"You're kidding me."

"No, honestly. I used to visit an elderly friend there. Sadly, she's dead now. She belonged to a spiritual movement called 'Subud', and lived in their Residential Home for the Elderly. It's in Frampton. You must have noticed it. It's called 'Wisma Mulia'. It's right by the bridge over the canal."

No, I'd never noticed it. And 'Wisma Mulia' – what sort of name was that!

"It's Indonesian, Wisma Mulia," he said, as if he'd heard my inner thoughts. "It means 'honour those who live here'. The man who founded the Subud movement in the 1930s was Indonesian, you see. If you're any sort of writer you should definitely visit Wisma. It's full of the most amazing characters."

The seed was sown. I had travelled six thousand miles to hear about somewhere literally on my doorstep back in Gloucestershire. This was meant to be!

On my return to England I telephoned the number Dimitri had given me, and was advised to call a second number to speak with David Barker. He told me how, in the 1970s, together with

Leonard Darlington and Leonard Openshaw-Stayner, he had formed a steering group with the aim of starting a care home for elderly Subud members.

David and his wife Emma were Subud members. He had received more than one indication, 'sign', even, that he should be starting a Subud Home, and that he should be searching in the county of Gloucestershire.

He did go there, but no property suggested itself as appropriate, and he moved his search elsewhere. But he had a recurrent dream in which he saw a lighthouse with GLOUCESTER painted on it. So eventually he returned to Gloucestershire.

This time he discovered the dilapidated but beautiful Georgian building that was to be modified and turned into Wisma Mulia, the only Subud Residential Home for the Elderly in the world at the time of writing. David persisted and saw the project through, creating Fountain Housing Association, which was to have charitable status.

Encouraged by David, I next rang Philip James, the Manager, and made an appointment. On the agreed day I made the twenty minute walk along the canal towpath and entered the house, having narrowly escaped injury by a resident emerging at a fair lick from the driveway astride her electric scooter, headed for the village Post Office. My interview was going well until Philip asked:

"And what exactly is it you want to do with the residents?"

I am not often tongue-tied. So certain had I been that Fate had decreed I work here at Wisma Mulia, I was expecting my role to have been decided for me also.

"Suppose I meet with the residents and ask them what they'd like?" I suggested.

"Good idea," said Philip. "I don't think there's any doubt you'd fit in here. I'm doing a barbecue on Tuesday. I'll arrange a Residents' Meeting for 11.00."

As the day approached, I prepared a brief introduction for myself, thinking vaguely of suggesting that people might like some sort of a reading group. Or to be read aloud to. On Tuesday at 10.50 I waited in the Garden Room, watching the residents arriving for the meeting.

Aged they may have been, but I'd rarely encountered a livelier bunch. Some twenty-five gathered, chatting nineteen to the dozen, from other parts of the main house, from flats in the wing, or from independent accommodation in the bungalow, Coach House or annexes around the gardens. All took their places. The nearest to me made polite conversation. Philip introduced the agenda and discussions began.

It took a long time, as everyone had an opinion. My impression was that I had arrived in a healthily busy community where the members wanted for nothing at all, and were not afraid to speak their minds, in the expectation that they would be listened to and their ideas and suggestions acted upon. The decor and ambiance were enchanting, activities abounded, residents were happy and fulfilled. Whatever else could I possibly contribute?

I made a feeble stab at presenting myself as a potentially useful person, and we all repaired to the garden for a splendid lunch. I took the opportunity to move from table to table, entering into conversation with each of them. I was closely questioned as to my background, where and how I lived, and whether I knew anything about Subud. Loans of explanatory books were offered. Patricia proposed to lend me a book she'd written herself about people's experiences of Subud. It was evident that many of them had known each other for years, through Subud, before ever they came to live at Wisma. These residents were vocal in expressing the pleasure to be had in living with a group of friends. Not every resident belonged to Subud. However, there was a particular atmosphere to the group that I had not experienced before. The place was alive, positively throbbing with good energy. I wanted to be part of it.

Mary, the Systems and Training Manager, gave me a full guided tour of the premises. I saw one of the empty flats, and had the annexed buildings pointed out to me. We moved briefly through the assisted bathing facilities, the hairdressing salon, the laundry room. I met the cheerful staff in the huge kitchen, whose door to the dining room apparently always stood open so that residents could look in. The dining room itself resembled a modest but tasteful restaurant, with its small tables for four laid with silverware, coloured tablecloths and linen napkins.

In the middle of the main building was a huge room, the Latihan Hall, in which Subud members worshipped, men and women attending separately. Apparently the Hall served also as a place for the Keep-Fit instructor to do his classes, a concert hall, a cinema and a training and meeting room. I saw the art room, to which an art teacher came once a week to work with interested residents. I was already familiar with the pretty Garden Room with its wicker furniture. The doors to the offices on either side of the front hall stood open invitingly. Attractive flower arrangements were to be found everywhere.

But it was the lounge that surprised me most. Situated to the left of the front door this sunny, pretty room had the air of a gracious drawing room in a family home. My recollections of the lounge in the (very expensive) nursing home in which my mother had died were painful. Though the Matron and staff there had been dedicated and well-qualified, nothing could disguise the sense of sadness, even hopelessness that assailed any visitor. The rows of sensibly 'wipe-down' upholstered, high-backed chairs lining the walls; the inevitable combined smells of cabbage and urine; the muted television in the corner, its images like permanent, moving wallpaper; above all, the silence, telling of despair and resignation – all were painfully etched on my memory. It had been a sorrow to enter its doors.

This lounge had a long window to the front garden, through which the sun poured, brightening the yellow-painted walls. Later I was often obliged to pull the curtains across this window so that my group members were not dazzled while we worked. French doors let onto another part of the garden, and an elegant fireplace and mantle occupied the third wall. A lovely gilt-framed mirror hung above the fireplace, and the pictures on the walls were attractive floral watercolours. There was a small television in one corner, but I was never to see it turned on.

The sofa and armchairs were deep and comfy, upholstered in a pretty fabric. There was a tapestried footstool, a side table with newspapers, a pot of pens and pencils and a thoughtful pair of all-purpose magnifying glasses for anyone who had forgotten theirs.

The room had a strangely dramatic effect on me. It was so ... homely. I was suddenly hit by a feeling of certainty. It was meant to be that I found my way to Wisma Mulia, and now I knew what I had to do there. The Community needed poetry.

This realisation was so sure, so big, that I didn't question where it had come from, nor ponder the fact that I had read no poetry for years, had ceased to write poetry in my thirties, and had no training in the teaching of poetry. It was simply a knowing, and I went with it. When asked the next time what I would be doing on my day at Wisma I answered confidently,

"I'm going to be running a Poetry Group!"

Chapter 2

Test Run

Why did I suggest a poetry group? Whatever possessed me? Philip and Mary would gaze at me sympathetically (or was it anxiously?) each time I emerged from the Lounge at noon on a Friday morning. A typical conversation would go like this:

"Any takers this week?"

"Oh, yes," I'd answer airily, trying to look more positive than I felt. "Jim stayed for half an hour, bless him. He'd told me he liked the *Rime of the Ancient Mariner*, so I brought that along."

Jim, a highly intelligent erstwhile Vicar, was invariably to be found in the lounge when I put in my appearance at 10.30. Thus, I had managed to hijack him for attendance at the so-called 'group', having cunningly tricked him into admitting a love of poetry.

"Someone lent me a wonderful version of the Ancient Mariner, with magnificent engravings by Gustave Doré," I went on. "Oh, and the girls brought Molly in." At 100, Molly was the oldest resident, an apple-cheeked, smiling poppet who was perfectly capable of carrying on a lucid conversation with you – when she wasn't asleep. "But don't worry! I'd come even if there was only one person interested."

My brave words belied my underlying nervousness. I'm used to making any of the projects I undertake a success, but this time things were looking distinctly wobbly.

"It might take a while to catch on," reassured Mary.

She was right. I had selected Friday morning as a rare free space amongst visits from the hairdresser, Keep-Fit classes, worship in the Latihan Hall, shopping expeditions, regular lunch appointments at the Bell (the local pub), sessions with the Art teacher or chiropodist, and the host of other regular activities arranged by the ever-energetic activities organiser, Jonsie. And still my attempts at 10.30 to round up people to come to the group were not meeting with very positive responses.

"Why would we want a poetry group?" asked Patricia, genuinely mystified. "I loathed poetry at school."

"I don't sink ve need a poetry group," stated Aine firmly in her still Germanic accent. "Ve're fah too busy!"

"I don't think it's for me, dear," said various others. Sometimes I managed to entice two or three to the lounge, where I would read them classic old favourites by the Romantics or the War Poets, or narrative poems like 'The Lady of Shallott' or sections of Rosetti's 'Goblin Market', and try to ascertain what they had enjoyed in the past so I could search out their requested poems for the following week.

Once captured and confined to an armchair, some of my reluctant visitors even admitted to having enjoyed their time with me. These weeks were the successful ones. But return visits made of the resident's own free will were not to be guaranteed, and my arts of persuasion would have to be brought to the fore once again the following Friday. I was definitely getting the feeling that Philip, Mary and other members of staff were beginning to think I was flogging a dead horse. Then the lovely Jim's attendances petered out. "I prefer to read poetry at my own pace," he excused himself tactfully, almost apologetically.

I couldn't explain, even to myself, why it was that I was persisting on my chosen course. It would be far easier to give it all up as a bad job. There was just this small voice that kept repeating, 'They need poetry – or some of them do. It's a primitive thing, this song with rhythm and rhyme. If you can just tap into it, something good will happen.'

So I kept on coming. I brought illustrated books of poems. I brought funny poems by Joyce Grenfell and Pam Ayres, and monologues by Stanley Holloway. I even brought limericks, in desperation. I tried to be more daring, and began to offer Ted Hughes, Dylan Thomas, D H Lawrence, Carol Ann Duffy. I even read one or two of my own poems. The responses began to be more animated, often dismissive or outraged, but at least energetic. We had one wonderful morning with a long debate about what, exactly, poetry was.

One day, 95-year-old Aine, who had been born and brought up in Berlin, told me that her favourite poet had been Rainer Maria Rilke. I went away and researched. I found a short poem in its original and with its English translation. During my next visit, I paid a call to Aine's flat and offered it to her. The following Friday she appeared in the Lounge at 11.00 sharp and took her place. I asked her to read the poem aloud to the rest of the group. She spoke it beautifully, with clarity, expressiveness and great sensitivity.

I then suggested that she read it again, this time in its original German form. The small group of listeners was visibly moved. At the end of the morning Aine said to me: "You don't haf to come to fetch me. If I'm coming, I'll be here."

She was as good as her word and became one of the staunchest core members of the Poetry Group – in spite of the fact that she was always short of time, because she was in the process of writing a book about her life!

Fiona began to attend regularly once she knew that I would be inviting members to read poems aloud themselves. One of the youngest members of the Wisma community at 64 (my own age), she still retained a Scottish burr in her voice, despite having spent much of her life speaking French while she lived in Tahiti. She read slow and sure, in a strong contralto voice. She was easily moved to tears by some poems, which gave rise at first to surprised comment from the others (never slow to voice an opinion!), leading us neatly into lively discussions about why poetry could affect us deeply, and what it was in a poem that could achieve this.

One week she arrived wearing an enormous red hat and a purple cardigan and proceeded to read 'When I Grow Old (I Shall Wear Purple)' by Jenny Joseph. The all-female group roared with laughter at this subversive take on an old lady's behaviour, especially the part that says she will spit, implying that no-one would have the nerve to do anything about it.

There was great delight all round and much applause.

The next week, doubtless inspired by Fiona's performance, Iris appeared with a book of poems about cats, beautifully illustrated. She presented it somewhat diffidently, but the group greatly enjoyed some of its contents.

Confident, outspoken and often mischievous Patricia, who had hated poetry at school, had taken to hanging around the Garden Room on a Friday morning at 10.45, much earlier than she usually got up. One Friday she announced that she'd "better come along to the Lounge, just to see what all the fuss was about." I felt this was a great mark of success. She stayed, about which no-one ever made any comment.

For months, she proclaimed that anything other than a light-hearted poem with a regular metre and rhyme pattern was 'far too araldite for me!', which naturally promoted laughter from the others.

But this assertion gradually died away, and she took to asking for explanations of the meaning of more difficult poems. She had usually asked the very question that everyone was wondering but not voicing, so our debates became the richer for it. There was many an argument about whether or not a poem needed to rhyme, with opinion shifting over time.

Another member who arrived at the outset, knowing that she enjoyed poetry and with such a zest for life that she enlivened every meeting, was Australian-born Maryse. She could be relied upon to turn up late, but with an Edith Evans-style flourish, often brandishing some random object – a length of beautiful Malaysian fabric she had picked up on her travels, or a book of funny quotations – which would inspire discussion and pleasure, and excite the memory of one more poem for me to bring along. Maryse's delight in the group was always evident, and she was often the first to thank me for spending my time there with them.

An energy was creeping in. Poetry always remained the main focus, but each member of the group gradually became a little more willing (and able) to share memories from the past. A fly on the wall might simply have seen a group of women chatting amicably and laughing a lot.

Over the months the group received numerous visitors, some who would have loved to have stayed but were only passing through Wisma Mulia for respite care, so couldn't, and some who came to try it but decided not to come back. Sometimes a visitor would say "I'll just sit here for 10 minutes", and could still be found there at the end of the session – and the start of the next. However, the core group settled into the following, and their ages in 2012 are:

    Aine – 97
    Fiona – 65
    Patricia –89
    Iris – 95
    Maryse – 86
    Other regulars who joined us over time were:
    Monica – 63
    Nancy – 77
    Naomi – 94
    Hosanna – 77

We started having to bring extra chairs into our comfortable lounge. By Christmas 2010 the Poetry Group was viable. There had been a dramatic improvement in each member's performance skills, and they looked forward to Fridays. It was a success.

Chapter 3

Settling In

Now that I could expect at least a handful of interested parties to turn up on a Friday morning, I developed the habit of arriving half an hour early and going to each of the ladies' rooms (other than Aine's, who, if you remember, did not want a reminder).

These visits became a privileged and intimate part of my time at Wisma. To be given permission to enter their private apartments and share a little of their individuality was a precious gift. Their personalities shone out from the very different ways in which they had equipped, decorated and maintained their living spaces, of course. I admired photographs of their loved ones, exclaimed over interesting objets d'art, and was treated to fascinating bits of history through pieces of furniture, books, pictures, documents, even clothing.

It was as if I had suddenly acquired another family, with all the richness that brings. No matter that sometimes one or two would have forgotten my name again; in the temporary absence of a name I was just the Poetry Lady, and always, apparently, welcomed.

"Oh, is it Friday? Good. How long have I got?" (Patricia, nowadays usually still in bed at 10.45 a.m.) Or "I've been waiting for you. Are we in the lounge?" (Fiona.) Or "How lovely to see you, sweetie. I'll just get my face on and join you." (Maryse, who would be at least another 45 minutes.) Or "Oh, I'm not feeling so good today." (Iris, who would get my answer – "You'd better get round to the lounge then, Iris! You know it will do you good." And it always did.)

Each week I'd try to come with something new in the way of a stimulus, as well as different poems for reading aloud. By this time everyone was happy to do the latter. I might suggest a poetry-related discussion, or the idea of posting a 'Poem of the Week' on a noticeboard somewhere for everyone in the house to read. I wanted poetry to become a living presence in Wisma Mulia. My idea of finding poems about trees and hanging them on threads from the branches of the huge magnolia tree outside the Garden Room (making it into a 'Poet-Tree') on the day of the Garden Party met with silence, and never happened. Sometimes I brought CDs of poetry spoken by well-known actors, though hearing problems provoked some comical misunderstandings from some of the members.

We made a 'Basket of Poems' for the lounge. The ladies suggested favourite poems, or selected from a supply I had provided for them to look through. I then wrote out the poems on separate pieces of coloured paper, rolled them up and tied them with ribbons. These were placed in a pretty basket with a notice pinned above it, inviting everyone to help themselves during a quiet moment – and then return the poem to the basket. As far as I am aware, not one was ever opened, the scrolls gathered dust, and I eventually removed them.

I was beginning to feel down-hearted again. Poetry just wasn't being noticed as a relevant, weekly activity at Wisma – except by my few newly-loyal members, and it felt as if it wouldn't be long before even they would start slipping away. It was becoming vital that I find a way for the group to begin to produce its own poetry. I was pretty sure what kind of alarmed response I would get if I proposed doing this, however.

Finally I hit upon a method of getting the ladies to 'write' their first poem, and in a completely non-threatening way. I selected some lines from poems by a number of writers, old and modern, and wrote them out on separate pieces of paper. There were two tenuous themes: 'evening' and 'winter'.

On September 3rd, after our usual preamble, I passed round the pieces of paper. Each person read their quotation aloud, and then a discussion was held. Hopeful as I had been about my little exercise, I could never have anticipated the vigour and interest of that morning's debates. I was completely taken aback by the vivaciousness of the comments, the opinions so clearly and strongly stated, the depth of understanding of the hidden meaning and poetic style evinced by the group members. By the end of the round some of the quotes had been irrevocably ditched by mutual consent.

We were left with a handful that everybody liked and was prepared to argue for, and these were placed on the floor in the middle of the carpet. A passionate argument ensued about just how they should be ordered to make a new, short poem. The result was the first poem 'constructed' by the Wisma Poetry Group. The words belong to TS Eliot, Alfred Lord Tennyson,

Ted Hughes and Edward Thomas. But the poem is ours. They called it 'Evening'. You can find it on page 37.

Hot on the heels of this success, the following week I suggested that we try to write a poem together using *their* words. We would call it 'Winter's Evening'. And it was during this session that the poetry-writing method we were to use frequently over the following 18 months began to emerge. First I would ask for any words or images attaching to 'evening' or to 'winter'. Everyone contributed, and I recorded everything faithfully in writing. A few leading questions from me, like 'What does that remind you of?' or 'How could you describe that colour more vividly?' or 'How could we turn round the words in that line to give a more satisfying rhythm?' began to elicit a more sophisticated poetic form. A final read-through allowed for last minute changes.

At home, I wrote out 'Winter's Night' (page 39) on black paper with a silver pen, and glued some silver stars in the top corners. It is still wedged into the bottom left-hand corner of the large mirror above the fireplace that I had admired on my first visit to Wisma Mulia.

Chapter 4

In Concert

One day, a notice in the hallway outside Philip's office caught my eye. It was inviting anyone who was willing to do a 'turn' at the Christmas Concert to sign up below. Half a dozen names were already inscribed. Enquiries of my ladies revealed that this annual event was always a popular occasion.

Samuel and Helena, who lived in the bungalow, had a son, Gregory, a successful actor currently touring with the Shakespeare's Globe Company. Clearly Helena, a once keen enthusiast of AmDram herself, had passed on some of her talent to her boy. Gregory, I was told, always arrived one or two days before the event and, seemingly miraculously, effortlessly put the concert together. It generally included 'The Wisma Anthem', (a humorous account of the goings-on of the mischievous residents, sung rousingly to the tune of 'John Brown's Body'); a dramatic piece, usually funny, read by his mother; various offerings from staff members; music and song by anyone willing, but most popularly by the Terrible Trio of Edward, David and Hassan and, if you were lucky, a Stanley Holloway monologue from the inimitable Philip. Villagers and relatives and friends were all welcome in the audience.

With the ladies' tentative agreement I signed 'The Poetry Group' at the bottom of the list. The Concert was the way to get us known about.

Over the next three weeks we worked hard to prepare a choral rendition of 'King John's Christmas'. Originally written for children by *Winnie the Pooh* author A A Milne, this is a deceptively clever story in rhyme about the not very nice King John, so unpopular that he has to send Christmas cards to himself. His only desire is for Father Christmas to bring him a great big red India-rubber ball. His wish comes true on Christmas morning, after a few anxious verses when we wonder if it will happen. Thanks be to my lovely ladies, none of whom ever questioned this choice of material or the decision to speak chorally, but just entered into the spirit of the thing with a will.

Please, dear reader, do not run away with the idea that any of my small ventures with the elderly community of Wisma Mulia went quite as smoothly as it may sound. Our rehearsals were beleaguered with continually lost practice sheets, requiring another painstaking marking up of that person's speaking part every time I provided a new copy; constant arrivals of members who suddenly discovered they had come without their reading glasses/hearing aid/pencil/handbag; continual reminders of why, how, where and when we would be reading 'King John's Christmas'. But my efforts were amply rewarded, not least in the dozens of times I heard "You're so patient with us, Steph."

Funnily enough, it didn't feel as if I was having to exercise patience. I was having such a good time, I sometimes wondered if I needed them more than they needed me.

The lovely Jim, one of the first to try out the group and then decide it was not for him, was always the first person I would have a chat with on arrival at Wisma on a Friday, thanks to his habit of sitting in the lounge with his post and the newspaper. He would carry on reading until everyone was assembled before departing to get on with his day. One day he had asked me if I could get hold of Oliver Goldsmith's 'The Country Schoolmaster', a poem he had much enjoyed in his youth. It was easy to find. I printed it out and he had seemed delighted.

Now, as we approached the time of the concert, it occurred to me that, having been a Vicar, and being possessed of an impressive baritone voice, Jim would make an excellent job of 'The Schoolmaster'. When I suggested this he seemed a bit bashful – but pleased to be asked. I mentioned it once or twice more as the day of the concert approached, and asked him to bring the copy with him on the night 'just in case'.

Gregory turned out to be the miracle-maker the ladies had described. With only two brief rehearsals (plus a wing and a bit of a prayer) the concert proved to be a splendid evening's entertainment, with many residents and staff alike demonstrating remarkable talent. Our 'King John's Christmas' was a triumph of synchrony, and was received with the hoped-for guffaws of laughter from all.

At one point in the programme, Naomi, from our Poetry Group, was listed as performing on the piano. From the start of the evening she had sat repeating under her breath 'I'm not going to play. I'm not going to play.' I reassured her that of course she wouldn't have to play if she didn't want to, but she remained quite anxious. She played beautifully, in fact, but rarely with an audience. When her spot in the programme came round and Gregory announced her name I called out that Naomi wouldn't be playing tonight, but that there was the possibility of a replacement item; I believed that Jim might have something he could do for us. To cries of encouragement, Jim rose, went to the lectern and proceeded to give a moving rendition of his poem. It was well received. After the Concert Jim asked me, 'Was it all right? Only I'd forgotten my hearing aid.'

This was to be the last occasion that the Poetry Group would meet until the third week of April 2011. I was, as always, flying out to Thailand for three months at the beginning of January. Over those intervening weeks, I was often assailed with worries and doubts. How would it be when I returned? With such a long gap, would I have to go back to square one and start encouraging everyone to come again? Would they all have forgotten me? Worse – what if any of them had died? Uncontemplatable! Would the Poetry Group be a thing of the past, my persistence wasted?

I reappeared at Wisma in April and started on my round of the ladies' rooms. All were healthy and well. And they remembered me. They told me how much both I and the poetry sessions had been missed, how they'd talked about it and waited impatiently for my return. They were ready and waiting in the lounge at 11.00 a.m. for the next phase to begin.

At the second meeting following my return, I adopted an expression of calm confidence and said:

"Well, I think you're all relaxed and confident with one another after all this time, and that the group feels like a safe, supportive place. So how about starting to write our own poetry, like we began to do last September?"

I waited for the cries of alarm. There were none. Instead, an exchange of glances, some nodding heads and then general agreement:

"Yes, why not?"

"How exciting!"

"We can give it a try."

At this point I was completely unsure how we would go about the process. I had to be careful not to put anyone on the spot; we were supposed to be having fun, not being made to feel uncomfortable. I was pretty certain that at least one or two of our members may have written their own poetry before. Aine, for example, who was currently in the process of finishing writing a book about her life in war-time Berlin and the subsequent years until she went to Australia. And Monica, who came to the group when her busy lifestyle allowed, used to be a University Lecturer in English – surely she was used to formulating poetry? But I wanted to aim for a group process, where the more able would support the rest and the outcome depended on a shared effort.

On May 6th I went to the meeting armed with an odd variety of items. I told the assembled company (which today included two new people, a gentleman and a lady not accustomed to coming to the Poetry Group) that we were going to write some poems that explored the senses – sight, touch, hearing, taste and smell. We were starting today with what we could see. Here were some objects to stimulate the sense of sight. I produced an old battered brown hat of mine; a small black china cat, curled up asleep; a bright blue glass bottle with a cork in it, and a few other objects.

The process went much the same as when we wrote 'Winter Evening': they needed prompting and pushing gently with questions to fully explore their imaginations, and the majority would work to support someone in the hot seat with ideas sometimes accepted and incorporated, more frequently scornfully rejected. Patricia chose to use her eyes upon the people sitting round the room, her friends. I can't remember whose idea it was to use the image of flowers to describe each one, but Patricia soon had the bit between her teeth and produced a striking piece of verse.

To my delight (and that of the group) I left that lunchtime with four poems recorded in my book. Was it always going to be this easy?

The answer was No. It was to be only infrequently that our poems wrote themselves so readily during a session. But a pattern began to develop in which I used our meeting times as opportunities to draw out words from the members – isolated words or phrases, whole accounts of a particular memory or musings stimulated by my questions and prompts or by the conversation on whichever topic I had proposed that day.

The surprising thing to me was that at home, when I laid out the writing, the poems seemed to sort themselves out in an almost magical way. Sometimes the words I had recorded verbatim appeared to fall into two or three distinct themes and these would make up two or three separate poems, often in dramatically different styles. Other times, every word I'd recorded just seemed to fall into place in a single poem. Rhythms came ready-made; I marvelled over this on many occasions. Rhyme followed close behind, sometimes internal to the poem, sometimes with the more predictable end-of-line patterns.

When friends suggested to me that this series of poems was actually my own and should be attributed to me, I hotly contested the idea. Assonance and alliteration, simile and metaphor, rhythm and rhyme were all there in my notebook before I ever left Wisma Mulia. These poems belonged firmly to the members of the Poetry Group. The most I could claim for myself was that I sometimes wrote a poem myself on the subject I'd chosen for a particular session. I would take this along as an illustration of one way of viewing the subject matter.

Yes, I did rearrange the order of the words the ladies gave me, and I did decide what didn't work and should be left out. But I steadfastly preserved their words.

I concede that much of the poetic process for the ladies was stimulated by me and by the way in which I presented the topics, enthused about them, gave examples from my own experience, demonstrated my own excitement for what we were talking about. Enthusiasm is catching. We can all remember a favourite teacher who somehow transformed something mundane into something magical. I was enjoying myself, feeling excited about the creativity evident in my group of very elderly women. After all, they had a lifetime's experience to share.

The exploration of the five senses proved fruitful material, although I was never able to make any poems at all from our two discussions about the sense of touch. Frustratingly, I was left with several pages of notes about the myriad things their hands had touched or felt during their lives – a sum total of almost 800 years of life between them, in fact.

It was astounding just how many poems were materialising. Every week the corridor wall was adorned with three, four, or even five brand new efforts, together with a brief explanation as to how they'd been arrived at. Jonsie suggested that we start printing out our poems on brightly coloured paper to make them more noticeable. Staff and visitors, as well as residents, began catching me as I moved through the building to tell me how much they were enjoying the poetry.

I arrived one Friday to be greeted by Cheryl, one of the care assistants. "We've got a surprise for you," she announced mysteriously. "I thought the Poetry Group should have its own proper noticeboard, now that it's a respectable weekly activity. So we've fixed one up for you in the Garden Room."

She took me to see it. It was a beautiful, long glass board in a frame. I would be able to write on and wipe off with a marker. A label in coloured capital letters across the top declared: POETRY GROUP. Two of the postcards I'd sent from Thailand were stuck in the corners, and the last session's poems were in the middle. Our own noticeboard! Now I knew the Poetry Group was really here to stay.

Chapter 5

Our Book

During the summer, the making of verse continued without cease. I began lying awake at night, reflecting on this ever-growing body of work. Yes, it always went up on display at Wisma each week, but surely it deserved a wider audience? Many of the poems abounded with joy, positivity and fun – a far cry from what tended to be the general conception of how old age manifests itself.

My amazing ladies (and occasional gentlemen) were not dessicated shells, sitting in a chair all day long in front of a television, passively giving themselves up to the indignities of helplessness. They were alive, bossy, vital, enthusiastic, argumentative and, above all, funny. What could I do to send out a message that old age can be a positive phase of life, and at the same time bring in some funds for Wisma Mulia, the place that had brought me so much?

And so the idea of our book was born. I approached the group with the idea of publishing their poems. They smiled, nodded and humoured me. So I pressed on. I shamelessly begged Philip for the capital outlay required for employing an editor/publisher who was experienced in the realm of self-publishing.

"No problem, go ahead!" was the answer.

Next, I ran the idea past Trish Mills, who already had a raft of high-quality self-published books under her belt, all of which were a bit different from the norm. She seemed enchanted with the notion of telling the story of the Poetry Group, read the poems and was moved, impressed. She took on the job (without charge, meaning we had to pay for the printing only), immediately providing me with invaluable information about formatting a book.

I introduced her to my ladies. She was wonderful with them, explaining processes clearly and patiently and engaging with them all skilfully, so that they took to her at once. The book became more real to them.

In May, a much loved resident and Subud member, Leila, died after battling with a long illness. Leila had been the instigator of the Wisma concerts and a major contributor to them. It was decided that a commemorative concert would be held in August to celebrate her life. Her husband, David, would give an address about her life and work. Any other contributions to the occasion would be welcomed.

I asked each Poetry Group member to select a favourite poem from our collection, and heard them read it aloud once or twice. Little formal rehearsal was required; they had become skilled performers. I met with Gregory and arranged our slot in the programme. The audience was larger than usual.

When it came to our turn, I gave a brief history of the group and described my plans for our book. The ladies then read their poems. Patricia was on first. She had chosen to read 'Ode to a

Hat', one of the very early poems. Irrepressible as ever, she insisted on donning a huge-brimmed, shocking pink hat for the performance, ignoring my protests that the audience wouldn't be able to see her face, and that, in any case, the hat in question was a battered old brown tweed version.

To add to the confusion, she had arrived without her reading glasses. I was obliged to stand at her elbow and hiss each line in turn at her, which she would then repeat. Sometimes she didn't quite catch what I'd said the first time, requiring me to repeat the line – the audience by then having heard it three times. It seemed doubtful that the message of this poem had come across at all clearly! In her mischief she wrought havoc with the little verse, but caused roars of laughter from the audience.

The other performers deported themselves more modestly, and I was conscious of the appreciative applause after each delivery. After the concert, I was besieged by people wanting to talk to me, to tell me how amazing they found the poems read that evening, to express excitement about the project, to suggest a book launch, or simply to tell me how much they had enjoyed the Poetry Group's inspiring contribution to the concert.

Margaret, Philip's wife (and, incidentally, Mary's sister), a Deputy Head Teacher of a local school, hoped she could bring some of her Year 6 children to meet up with the ladies, just to see what came of it. Of course, I said yes.

The weekly work continued. The stock of poems grew. Philip purchased a tiny voice recorder so that I could record a personal interview with each of the core members. (These can be found on page 115, after the poems.)

In November, as arranged, Margaret arrived at one of the Friday meetings with some of her 10- and 11-year-old pupils. We met in the Latihan Hall, the Lounge not being large enough. As often happens when the young meet the old, there appeared to be no barriers to animated conversation between the two factions.

After our project had been explained to the children, I read them one or two of the poems we had written in preparation for their visit, and we discussed some of the references to the past which they may not otherwise have understood (the mysterious 'Liberty bodice', the old money system in shops with overhead wires to the cashier's box, and so on).

A long 'argument' was then documented on the relative advantages and disadvantages of being 10 in 2011 versus the 1930s.

Everyone appeared to have enjoyed the encounter very much indeed. As the children departed, one was heard to comment:

"I think I'm going to retire early and come and live here. It's cool!"

In December I decided to lead the group in an experiment with a different poetic approach. I chose the Haiku, a Japanese poetic form. It is difficult to make an English Haiku in exactly the same way as it works in Japanese, where the 'ons', or sound bites (nearest equivalent in English, syllables) are different. The form is completely rule-bound.

It must be like a snapshot of a single, transitory moment, usually depicting something in nature. It must have a seasonal element, if not named, at least suggested. There must be two discrete ideas contained within it, separated from each other by punctuation, usually a dash, a colon or an ellipsis (three dots ...) And there must be only three lines. The first line should contain five syllables, the second seven, and the last five, making a total of 17 syllables.

I was excited by my idea, but a little concerned about having to explain so many rules to the ladies in the hope that they would remember everything. For the first time in the group's history, I equipped myself with a whiteboard and a marker and began to 'teach'. How would this be for those who 'hated poetry at school' I wondered. I wrote up the example I had written for the session, 'The Swan', and started my exposition. Ten minutes in, I examined all the faces. They were rapt. Sensible questions were asked. Volunteers put themselves forward and gave remembered 'snapshots'. The group corrected syllable counts, reversed word orders and helped polish up. By the end of the session we had two Haiku. The ladies arrived a little early the following Friday, impatient to continue with our experiment in writing Haiku. By the end we had five.

At Gregory's Christmas concert for 2011, I was not about to give away any more of our material. We wanted everyone to buy our book, after all. The group put in an appearance, however, with a hearty choral rendition of Pam Ayres' 'Oh, I Wish I'd Looked After Me Teeth', together with one or two poems about the end of one year and the start of a new one. It had been far easier this time to get Jim involved; he accepted my suggested poem by Robert Service without demur, and gave a quite splendid, meaningful performance, as I had expected. I thought of him as a kind of Honorary Member of the Poetry Group.

Now it was time to say goodbye once again. I was flying out to Thailand for my usual three months in mid-January. But this time, armed with a large notebook, a sheaf of precious poems, the recordings of the ladies' interviews and a computer, I had my holiday task planned. The writing of our book. By my return mid-April it was to be ready for editing and would then go to print!

Chapter 6
The Poems

WHAT'S IN A POEM?

It pares down the story to leave just the nub,
The essence, the kernel, the heart of the thing.
Mysterious expression with rhythm and rhyme,
It has shape on the page – a song we can't sing.

It may come with an impact, a drum roll, a shout,
A rainbow explosion, a thunderbolt's fright.
It may slide up all sinuous, a goldfish in reeds,
Float like a woman who dances the night.

A glimpse of a memory that's come from the past –
A window just opened, a door that's ajar,
Showing us beauty or sadness or fear,
Excitement or courage or shangri la.

Its images are various, powerful, clear –
A peacock in splendour, someone waving goodbye,
A veil on a pale cheek, a dahlia in bloom,
The face of a child who's beginning to cry.

A poem is serious, quirky or fun,
Melodious, staccato, wistful or glum,
Cheeky, sarcastic, heroic or rude,
Longish or shortish or just as they come.

A rhythm's what shapes it and pushes it on,
Like hooves as they gallop, the clock's ticking hand,
The beating of tom-toms, our feet as they dance,
The march of the soldiers, the Saturday band.

A poem is something that's deep in our soul.
It's planted within us, set there in the past.
It's food for our dreaming, it makes us all whole,
It answers the questions we don't know we've asked.

Although this poem was not written until 16th September 2011, it seems a very fitting opening to the collection.

3rd September 2010

In the early days of the Poetry Group I introduced our first exercise to encourage the writing of poetry.

We shuffled some striking lines from other people's poems, famous people's poems. I had written these on separate pieces of paper, which I handed round to everyone. Two main themes figured in the quotes: 'Evening' and 'Winter'.

The ladies then read out in turn the line/lines they had been given. Discussion took place about the merits or otherwise of the piece and the quotation was either retained or rejected. The surviving papers were placed in the middle of the carpet, and a long time elapsed while the ladies argued vociferously about which should go into the poem and which shouldn't, and how the winning lines should be ordered.

The following rather beautiful verse was the end result. Of course, we have to thank these poets for the words themselves:

> T S Eliot
> Ted Hughes
> Alfred Lord Tennyson
> Edward Thomas

But the poem is ours.

Evening

Now the hedgerow is blanched for an hour
With transitory blossom of snow.
A cool, small evening, shrunk to a dog-bark
And the clank of a bucket,
Twilight, and evening bell
And, after that, the dark.
The hour between the far owl's
Chuckling first soft cry
And the first star.

10th September 2010

Inspired by the construction of 'Evening' when we used the words of other poets, today the Poetry Group wrote their own poem evoking a snowy, English night.

Winter's Night

Winter, and the snow is white

Strange forms folding, glimmering

Snowflakes, feathers from Mother Goose's pillow

Diamond stars in an obsidian sky

Icicles on the gutterings dripping and squeaking

Scream of a vixen on the wind

Cat creeping, barn-owl sailing

Silence

6th May 2011

With the intention of exploring each of the five senses in verse, today the group began with the sense of SIGHT. As a whole group we first practised our powers of observation with one of Steph's favourite old hats, a battered tweed affair used when boating in the rain.

Ode to a Hat

How I love thee,
Battered old comforter.
My thanks to you,
Old friend.

Not elegant or à la mode,
Not smart, not Ascot.
You are no fascinator.
But you've been with me

In rain, snow, wind and fog
Long years.
Mine forever.

Next, the group supported Patricia to write a poem about all the friends she could see seated in the room with her. She decided to use the image of flowers to describe everyone. We also had the chance to compare metaphor and simile in our discussions.

My Friends

Maryse
Full-blossomed lady,
Like the wild
white lilac.

Iris
Of the aquiline face
In her beautiful blue
Devoré blouse,
An iris, indeed.

Nancy
In her fancy blue,
A hydrangea,
Queen of the garden.

Steph
Delicate and fine
Like the white
magnolia.

Fiona
The Red Hot Poker.

Eve, Gypsophila
A froth of white,
So delicate, so hazy.

Albery
Noble laurel
Without his Hardy.

What a lovely bunch!

To practice her powers of observation and put them into a lyrical form, Fiona chose a small, black china cat, curled up in a ball fast asleep. She is fond of cats, having one of her own, called Becky. You may remember the striking description of the curve of the cat's hip when you come to read my interview with Fiona about her life.

Black Cat

Sleepy, lucky black cat,
Dozing on the cane chair
In a patch of sun
Below the lilac tree.

Your ear twitches.
Are you chasing flutterbies,
Field mice or dry leaves
Blowing in the wind?

Curled up tight,
A ball with ears.
Tiny little wet snub nose,
Tail wrapped round you
Like a woolly scarf.
One hip in the air,
The hip of a Tahitian girl
Dancing.

You will read in my interview with Maryse of her fascination in discovering the details of how her Huguenot ancestors started the famous factories that made – and still make – the beautiful blue glass so representative of Bristol.

Obviously, her eye was drawn to a curious blue glass bottle with a cork in the top. Here are her observations.

Blue Bottle

Bottle blue
Beautiful hue,
Reminds me of sea.

Where have you come from?
What have you been?
Have you carried
An exotic perfume
Speaking of foreign lands,
Strange places, different faces?

You have me dreaming.

I shall fill you full
Of Eau de Voyage
And together we'll go
To that next mirage.

13th May 2010

The group now turned its attention to the sense of TASTE. This was an extremely popular session, since I had brought along a number of exciting foodstuffs to stimulate our taste buds. The enjoyment with which these were received was definitely reflected in the resulting poems.

We were obliged to move our session into the Garden Room so that we could all sit round a large table and not make too much mess. Consequently, we had a number of interested visitors dropping in, who shared the pleasure of some of our tastings as well as adding in a small way to the making of our verses. I think you'll agree that the following selection of poems actually makes one salivate! Job well done . . .

Kiwi

There are memories of France,
Country of adored kiwi vines.

Like a giant gooseberry,
Clothed in a dark, hairy skin,
Brown, unlovely – but holding delights within!

A creamy centre to the pellucid green flesh,
A perfect circle of unexpected
Black seeds that catch in your teeth.
Crisp or slushy to the bite,
Some flavoured water with pips,
Sweet and strange.

Crunchy Bars

They all bite.

There is silence.

The improbable sweetness
Has gripped each one.

Look at their faces,
Wrapping their mouths
Around the chocolate,
Teeth first efficiently
Pulverising the melting
Honeycomb:
Then glued together
In helpless surrender.

Silence . . .

Pretzels

Salty little beasties, aren't they?
Looped into hearts, they crunch,
Get stuck in your teeth,
Explode their rock salt granules
Against your palate.
Crushed into atoms
Of pressed cardboard flavour
They encourage me to drink more.
An American invention
Of dubious character,
The bar-tender's friend.

Turkish

In your half-crown balsa box,
full of Eastern promise,
you are the pretty, poor relation
of the sugar-dusted sweetmeat
silver-salvered in an Ottoman tent
or in the cool halls of harems.

There was a sprawling nunnery
that clung tight to craggy cliffs
above an indigo, flashing sea,
in whose dim and reverent rooms
I sat beside an ancient Grecian nun,
rook-black-cowled and kindly faced.

A silent hour of curious awe, it was.
Her smile was old as the Parthenon

Delight

when she rose to lift and offer me
with wordless grace a lidded dish
on which lay piled the powdered squares,
dawn pink and lemon yellow.

I took the gift between my fingertips.
My teeth sank sticky through the cube
and powdered sugar clothed my lips
then melted like the snow.
There was attar of roses upon my tongue
and in my nostrils.

It seemed the perfumes of the Orient
were in my mouth, with the sweet
spirit of that Grecian nun
who offered an hour and Turkish Delight.

This was my example poem, brought to the group at the start of our 'Taste' session. It is the account of an actual experience of mine.

We have Nancy to thank for her charming evocation of a scene in her childhood kitchen, and Maryse for her erudition in being able to explain to us all the origins of the famous St Augur, in the following poem.

Blue Cheese from St Augur

Nancy's thinking of her Dad,
Liked Gorgonzola from the market.
Sitting in the old wooden carver
At their kitchen table
In his brown farmer's smock,
Sliding it into his mouth
From the end of his knife.

Now, we eat the svelte
And gentle St Augur.
Slippery, tangy, creamy-sweet,
It slides over the tongue,
Barely touching the teeth,
To titillate the tonsils.

Cave-made cheese, sent
In baskets up the Pyrenean
Mountainside, to feed
French Papal escapees,
Here sits on a Frampton table.

27th May 2011

Week 3 of our writing about the five senses found us attempting to evoke sounds. It wasn't quite as simple as we thought. Here is the result of a collective brainstorm:

Sounds We Love

Promising hiss and gurgle of the Gaggia coffee machine,
Splutter of the liquid splashing into the cup.

Pop of the toaster offering up a golden slice.
Hiss and crackle of the egg broken into hot fat.

Thunder of breakers on a windswept pebble beach,
Protesting rattle of stones dragged back with the surf.

Soughing and rustling of Springtime breezes
Playing hide-and-seek in the acacia tree.

Interminable jovial conversation of jackdaws
Discussing village affairs – such gossip!

Deep, satisfying absence of sound
Under a dark, star-filled sky.

Maryse offered we European folk an unusual array of sounds, recalling her Australian origins:

Sounds of the Outback

Out at our sheep station,
Late at night,
Footsteps on the verandah.
'Jack, Jack – bring the gun!'
Silence once again.

Morning comes, announced
By the double click of shears
Clipping away a fleece.

Happy kookaburras
Chortle in the gum tree,
Till a howling wind brings
A sudden dust storm,
Turning the sky red.

Nancy was brought up on a farm and her memories provided all the rich material necessary for this poem.

Daybreak at Milton End Farm

The cockerel was our alarm clock,
With his hoarse, arrogant crowing.
Then birdsong from under the eaves
And across in the woods.
Cows lowed in the milking parlour
Giving up their creamy stream.
The new-fangled John Deere tractors rumbled past,
Too fast.
The snuffle and grunt of the pigs,
Nellie pushing her bowl across the cobbles
As she licked the last morsel –
All told me it was time to get up.
Downstairs in the kitchen,
Music on the radio accompanied
Mum's clanging of the pans on the Rayburn
And the cheerful whistle of the boiling kettle.

In stark contrast to this English scene, here is a brief poem I wrote in Thailand.

Cleaning

In England my cleaning
Is a feverish thing.
The hoover pants and barks,
A terrier rushing to and fro
Across the carpet,
Excited, ravenous, indiscriminate,
Gobbling morsels of rubbish,
Clawing at invisible marauders.
It is a task to hurry,
Get done with, quickly, quickly.
Then the machine swallows
Its cable, loop by loop,
And goes back into its kennel.

*In Thailand I sweep.
I swing the light bamboo cane
In swishing arcs,
A horse's tail, lazily
Flipping this way,
Flopping the other.
Cooly over the pale tiles
The fan of fronds gently
Shifts the dust, the sand,
Small corpses of mosquitoes,
A silent sacrament
To the heated day.*

3rd June 2011

No-one seemed to be getting bored yet. Our task for today was to get to grips with the tricky task of bringing the sense of smell alive on the page. We plunged our noses into an array of pots, jars and boxes that I had brought with me.

Then enthusiastic conversation recalling our youth broke out. Everyone was agreed on just how powerful a single aroma can be in transporting us back in time to a particular place.

Here are the results.

Smells We Have Loved

As they recall those scents that filled
The airs of childhood long ago,
Their faces smooth and soften,
Eyes look up, away,
And everybody smiles.

They tell of summer's apple smell
With orchards heavy-hung with fruit.
And when sand and salty sea
Were family picnics' condiment –
Chequered tablecloth and laughter
When sand got in the sandwich.

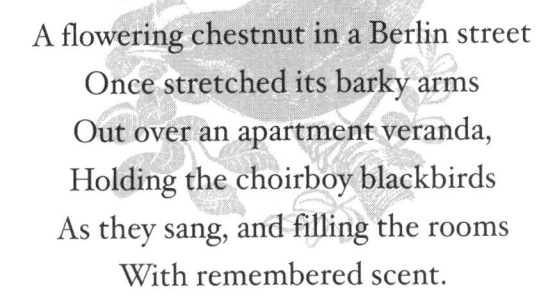

A flowering chestnut in a Berlin street
Once stretched its barky arms
Out over an apartment veranda,
Holding the choirboy blackbirds
As they sang, and filling the rooms
With remembered scent.

Some screw up their noses, others laugh,
At the fierce, robust and piercing smell
Of Marmite – hated, loved.
Burnt sugar on an electric stove
Means blackcurrant jam-making
To one, and then a string
Of other odours come:
Tomatoes in a greenhouse
Puffed with DDT. Geraniums,
Fried bacon, garden mint,
Nutmeg, cloves and Christmas pine.

Thanks be for noses large and small,
Snubbed, aquiline or broad,
And all the riches they provide.

As we read the next poem, it's clear that we oldies cling to the idea that English summers are still reliably hot and heady. It was largely inspired by this myth and by the wonderfully tended, flower-filled gardens of Wisma Mulia.

England in Summer

It is, indeed, an idyll,
This land of ours in June.
Brief rainfall leaves the air
Thick with the heady smell
From froths of elderflower
And sweet, potent honeysuckle
Trailing in the hedgerow.
Lavender, squeezed between fingers,
Gives up its spicy oil,
And bees bounce
In the spiky stems, ecstatic.
The mower in the distance hums
And smell of new-cut grass
Is set adrift to lull us back
To childhood, when shirt-sleeved Dads
Push-pulled, push-pulled
To mow the homely lawn.
The temptress perfume of the rose
Bids us press our nose
To the damp velvet and inhale
As deep as dilating nostril will allow,
And steep our spirit in the glory.

Here is a memory of my own.

Toast

Comforting smell of freshly-made toast
Curls unexpected out of the kitchen.
I am back on my Grampy's knee
Where – bald head shining –
He sits in his brown wing-back chair,
Face glowing in demonic red light
From the three-bar electric fire.
In my small hand the toasting fork
Is a brass shaft of wonderment,
The thick white slice impaled,
Submitted to the torture of Hellish fire,
Slowly turning ribby-golden,
Drying out,
Giving up its fleshy moisture
In the daily sacrifice.

This is a humorous take on the admonition of our mothers that many of us remembered – never wear too much perfume!

Wearing

"Just put a little behind each ear,"
Mother always impressed.
"And a soupçon dabbed upon the wrist;
The pulse will do the rest."

We've shampooed our permanent wave,
Bathed, shaved and taken a nap;
For this is how women behave
When they're planning to capture a chap.

We've zipped up the slim pencil skirt,
We've straightened our immaculate seams,
We've tucked in the crisply starched shirt,
For we're hunting the man of our dreams.

Perfume

Our ear-rings and necklace in place,
Our feet squashed into high heels,
Padded shoulders we finally brace,
For each one truly womanly feels.

But wait! (there's a sense of alarm),
Something is missing, I fear,
That 'Je ne sais quoi' that will charm –
It's a dab of it under each ear!

Is L'Aimant by Coty too sickly?
Or Evening in Paris too loud?
We want to feel sexy, and quickly,
And float to that dance on a cloud.

24th June 2011

In June, I felt a change of direction was required. Today's session took place in the Garden Room, again due to the need for a table. The ladies arrived to find an upturned metal roasting tin in each person's place, over the surface of which magnetic words clung.

"We are going to liberate our minds from the burden of logical thought for a change," I announced firmly, as confused questions began to bubble up. "The words in front of you are randomly selected. There is no pattern, no theme, and there are very few 'little' words, such as 'and' or 'the'. This means you won't be able to make complete sentences in the usual way.

"Please simply select any words that particularly claim your attention. Don't attempt to link them together; just choose words that interest you."

Oh, what a pleasurable morning we had! The ladies soon got the idea that they needed to select the words that fascinated, appealed, amused or impacted upon them. Having made their choices, we had a rollicking time shuffling and rearranging them, sometimes combining two or three choices into a larger selection.

From these groups of disconnected words the following poems emerged. Some of the traditionalists were not too sure about all of the results but, on the whole we agreed they all seem to have an immediacy and quirkiness difficult to produce when we put words together in a more routine, expected way. I am obliged to my good friend, Richard Conlon, for the idea of this very creative exercise.

How economically this pretty poem evokes the start of a day near a lake.

Morning Birds

Smoky; bird; morning; chatting; velvet;
cloud; lake; wild; kiss; far; seek.

Smoky velvet cloud kisses the lake.
Small morning birds chat,
Seeking near and far
Fierce, wild blackberries,
Fat, juicy rowanberries,
Early, unfortunate worms.

You may not agree that a 'paradise of children's voices' amounts to an accurate description, but who could argue against the perfect conjunction of 'candy' and 'cliff'?

Birthday Rain

children; always; voice; paradise; cliff; celebrate; rain; swim; rainbow; eternity; roundabout; birthday; laughing; candy; river

The ground was hard and parched.

On a birthday roundabout

A paradise of children's voices

Celebrated the arrival of rain,

A laughing rainbow river

Swimming into eternity

Under the candy cliff.

The name of the lady in the next poem was suggested by Nancy, who named her own daughter thus. We wonder what her dream could be . . .

June

embrace; brilliant; happy; blush; dream; queen; flood; ribbon

June, blushing happily,

Embraces her dream

At the flooding ribbon of river,

Feels the brilliant day.

She is Queen of the May.

I was challenged by the group with an apparently awkward and unpromising list of words they had chosen for me. However, this poem evolved easily and fluidly and just happened to fit the thread of the title that Iris had suggested.

Here and There

river; present; donkey; slow; young; afternoon; embrace; vast; memory; laugh; squirm; circle

In the slow afternoon
Two young lovers embrace.
He laughs. She squirms.
In the vast circle of the valley
They lead their donkey
Down to the river to drink,
Making another memory ready
For when today's present
Becomes the future's past.

Autumn

9th September 2011

On a beautiful sunny day we gathered our recollections of Autumns past. This first poem may not rhyme in any obvious way, but the busy pace and the lack of end-of-line punctuation speed us on like a gusty wind.

Let's go foraging
While the wind is scurrying
Let's pick blackberries
Hips and haws, damsons, sloes
Let's search for nuts and seeds
Harvest apples, marrows, plums
Let's kick up all the leaves
Smell the wholesome earthy tang
See the woodland cyclamen
Glimpse azure sky through golden tree
Puff-ball cloud and thistle seed
Let's clothe ourselves in red
Russet, orange, golden, lime
Let's stride out through the wind
Glory in the Autumn time!

Autumn was not the favourite season for every group member, as it reminded them of the winter to come. The next poem is a very evocative picture of the 'burnt-out end' of the season, when skies are getting grey and everything is muffled, damp and misty. (Personally, I love it!)

Autumn Draws to a Close

Lapwings call above the red ploughed fields
Herons stand like lampposts down the banks
Cows appear to swim in pools of mist
Dewdrops be-jewel spiders' crocheted webs

Thunder rolls behind the leaden sky
Wind holds its breath and waits its turn
Rain drips on sodden mats of leaf
Crows call like ratchets past the hedge

Frilled toadstools sprout from rotting logs
Coils of acrid smoke from bonfires seep
Gaudy pumpkins sag upon the vine
Kitchen-garden scarecrows stand asleep

Lastly, in our poems for Autumn, a light-hearted reminiscence of the two ways we think about the miracle of Horse Chestnuts.

Horse Chestnuts

Push the smooth and burnished spheres
Out of their velvet beds.
Rub them in your palms,
Warm, polished mahogany.
Line them up in rows on windowsill and shelf.
Admire their individual tilt,
The small window of light on each
Companionable, chocolatey face.
Cushion them gently in a pocket,
Fill bowls and baskets with them.
Be kind to chestnuts.

BAKE THEM IN THE OVEN'S VIOLENT HEAT,
SOAK THEM IN A VINEGAR BATH.
DRILL HOLES SAVAGELY THROUGH THEIR HEARTS
AND PUSH THROUGH A STRING
WITH A KNOT AT THE END.
AWARD EACH ONE A STATUS.
WHIRL THEM DANGEROUSLY ROUND YOUR HEAD.
SWIPE ONE AGAINST ANOTHER MURDEROUSLY.
SMASH THE RIVALS INTO WHITE SMITHEREENS.
BE PROUD OF CONKERS.

30th September 2011

Everything is not always plain sailing in the Poetry Group. After all, I'm only human, and my judgement is often a bit astray.

On this Friday, I thought that my old sewing box would stimulate wonderful memories. In fact, it seemed the majority of the group members couldn't stand sewing!

So here is my sheepish account of our session.

The Work Box

"I'll take them my lovely old work box!
It's bound to unlock lots of things.
I'll spill out the contents to show them –
The needles, the scissors, the pins.

"I'll pull out the spools of bright cotton,
Trail scarlet and emerald and blue.
They'll trigger the memories forgotten
Of sewing they once used to do.

"The bindings and curls of elastic,
The thimble, the threader, the chalk,
The beads, pinking shears (so fantastic!),
Will stimulate hours of talk.

"They'll remember their Grannies and mothers,
Children's costumes devised for a show,
The dress that they made for a party;
The pleasure will make faces glow!"

But this time I'm wholly mistaken,
I've got it entirely wrong.
When I take out my work box to show them
Their faces are frowning and long.

"But why would we be fond of buttons?"
"Elastic's for knickers, that's all."
"I hated my school sewing lessons:
I completed nothing at all."

"I'd throw something into the dustbin
To avoid sewing button or stud!
My mother was like it before me –
I think it must run in the blood."

Just one person looks at me, smiling,
Says, "I like sewing, I have to confess.
I taught myself slowly, and later
Produced my own wedding dress."

28th October 2011

  The group had spent some time preparing for the proposed visit of Margaret's seven Year 6 children to a Poetry Group meeting. We thought a suitable theme for discussion would be what it was like to be aged 10 in the 1930s compared to being aged 10 in 2011. We produced four separate poems, just from the eager and fulsome reminiscences of being a child in the twenties and thirties (or, for some, the forties and fifties).

  Here is a joint memory of going to the local shop (in someone's front room) and choosing sweets for very little money, which were then put into a screw of newspaper. Will the children know about 'old' money – a threepenny bit, tuppence and a halfpenny? (We couldn't get the sixpence or the farthing in!) The nature of the sweets themselves doesn't seem to have altered at all.

Sweets

Going up to the top shop
I've got threepence to spend!
I can buy five different things
And still have a halfpenny to lend.

Black Jacks and aniseed balls
Laces of liquorice coiled
Sherbet dabs and humbugs
Sweets squidgy and fizzy and boiled.

The shop is a cottage's parlour
Its door straight onto the street;
My sweets are put in a newspaper cone
Screwed up at the bottom all neat.

Going up to the top shop
I've got threepence to spend!
I can buy five different things
And still have a halfpenny to lend.

There are one or two things in this way of shopping that won't be recognised by today's youth. It's not quite a trip to the Mall. Will they be surprised by the mention of Sainsbury's, we wonder . . .

Shopping

Oh, I remember all of us
Climbing into the Governor's cart
On a Friday morning. Snap went the reins
And the pony trotted us all the way
To Mr Hazel, the Grocer.

Oh, I remember Sainsbury,
The marble counter, bacon slicer,
The cashier prim in her high box
Looking down on us below,
Rapunzel in her counting house.

The shop lady put our money and a bill
Inside a wooden acorn. Away it whizzed,
Trundling on cables across the ceiling
To the posh cashier in her tower.

If she liked you
She'd send you back some change.

Not a lot about school has changed, except maybe corporal punishment and Spam unrelated to a computer.

School

Head teacher whisking by. Flapping in his black gown
'Bat man, Bat man' we whisper, giggling.

I'd rather stand in the corner, Face to the wall for an hour,
Than feel the rap of a ruler, Feel the slap of a slipper,
Feel the sting of the thin cane, Feel the cat o' nine tails.
I'd rather write a hundred times, 'I must behave, I must not talk.'

My desk has a scarred and ancient lid, An inkwell at the top. I dip my pen
And blackness seeps all over my fingers And under my nails.

At eleven o'clock we all have milk. The tiny bottles have sat like dwarves
In a crate in the classroom since eight. The milk is warm. I feel sick.

Hopscotch in the playground,
Grandmother's footsteps, skipping games.
Mothers and Fathers behind the hedge.
Perhaps we'll have Spam for dinner!

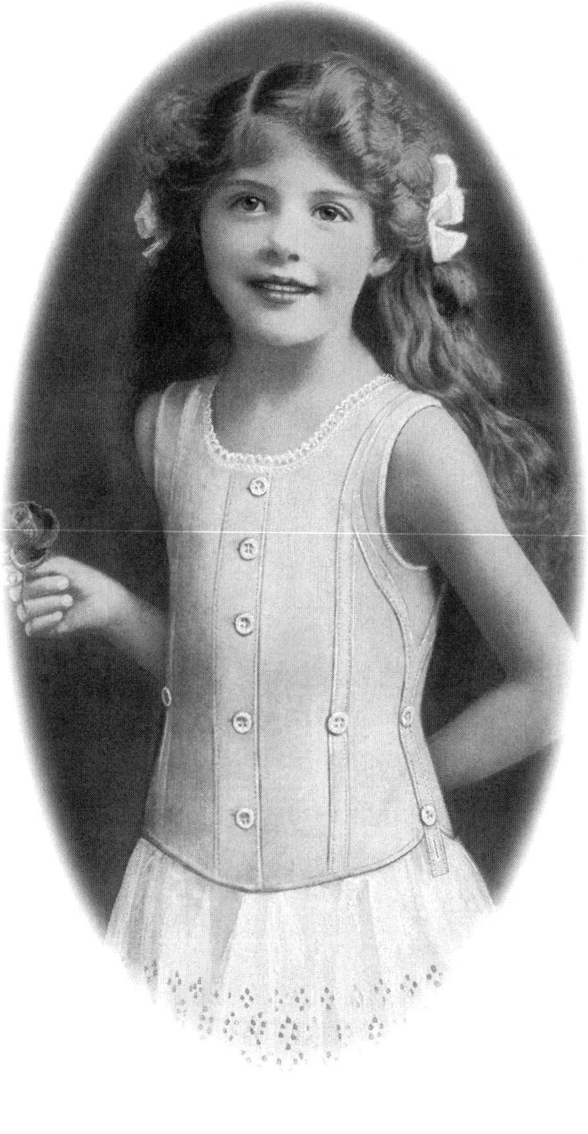

I suspect this will *really* fox the children and will need careful description and explanation!

Liberty Bodice

Mother is worried that winter cold
Will carry me off with the 'flu.
So Liberty Bodice, Liberty Bodice,
(Who the hell called it a Liberty Bodice?)
Nicely padded and tightly fit,
Canvas buttons you struggle to fix.
Over combinations and stockings of lisle,
(If any boy saw you he'd run a mile!)
All reeking of menthol that Mother's rubbed on
(From a jar of Vicks Vapour rub it has come –
It makes your eyes water, the fumes are
so strong!)
The Liberty Bodice is my winter friend
And I'll wear it stoically right up to the end.

In December 2011 we learned about the Japanese poetic form, Haiku. For the first time, I used a whiteboard, worried that the atmosphere in our comfy lounge might be spoiled by this return to the days of school lessons, the teacher writing on the blackboard about boring subjects.

I need not have worried. My lively-minded audience paid close attention, absorbing the numerous rules bounding this tiniest of poetic styles. 3 lines, 17 syllables (5 for the first line, 7 for the second, another 5 for the last), a seasonal reference, a 'cut' somewhere, dividing the first thought from a second, a 'snapshot' feel of a single, perfect moment in nature – but packing some emotion.

Trying them out for ourselves confirmed the amount of precision and thought required to produce this 3-line oeuvre – the frustration and joy of Haiku!

When we had looked at some translations of Japanese versions, I offered an example of my own, The Swan. The group then helped with the construction of Haiku about remembered moments from Maryse, Iris and Aine. Lastly Monica suggested something more modern and 'gritty', and she and Hosanna wrote the last one together.

THE SWAN
moon-white swan gliding
on the lake's night-black water:
proud winter ice queen

FLOWER DELIGHT
Japanese tea bar
lotus with pebble and leaf –
my tranquility

LADYBIRD
scarlet ladybird
round, cheery, autumn mother –
fly back to my home

RAINBOW
July rainbow glows:
white doves' sudden sweep under,
glinting in the sun

WINTER WAITING
shivering bus queue
where the homeless are sleeping...
breath steams in the air

The group and I frequently talked about 'a sense of time', almost as if it were a sixth sense, and, indeed, it is something key to anyone in the closing stages of their life. The single poem I've selected from that work was written on August 19th 2011, but seems just right to close this section of poems devised by the group as a whole.

Prayer for Old Age

*Tempus Fugit – nothing halts
Its passage, be it fast or slow.
Minutes, seconds, ticking, tocking,
Round and round the clock-face
Revolve the relentless hands
Marking, in their perpetual movement,
Our journey towards our Maker.*

*And here we are together
In the last stage, the final chapter,
The evening of life, the end,
The Grand Finale – looking
Over the fence to see
What's on the other side.
Ever noticing our good fortune
To be in this place and in this faith.*

Our thanks for those who care,
Respectfully and cheerfully,
To benefit our lives.

Wisma Mulia: honoured home.
Our thanks for the pleasure of friendship,
Shared food, laughter, reminiscence,
The lively mind, the busy day.

Our thanks for this garden
And its daily song of joy.

Our thanks for this building,
Sunny rooms and pleasant aspects.

Our thanks for the peace of mind
We are gifted for this final episode.

And let us keep our sense of wonder,
Curiosity, excitement, vivacity and mischief.

Members' Earlier Poems

As I had suspected, some of our group members had indeed written poetry in the past.

The following poems have been offered to us for the Wisma collection by Aine Branting, Hosanna (Emily) Kingston and Monica Jones, for which we are most grateful.

Aine's Poems

As you will read in Aine's fascinating interview, she lived for many years in Jakarta. She has kindly allowed me to include in this book two delightful poems she wrote whilst there.

In the Streets of Jakarta 1

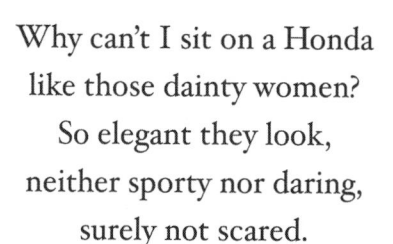

Why can't I sit on a Honda
like those dainty women?
So elegant they look,
neither sporty nor daring,
surely not scared.

Their nimble bodies relaxed,
their faces soft and gentle
as they hold on
to their mate in front.
They look like sitting in an armchair,
slim legs stretched to one side,
a shoe dangling,
with perfect poise.

So calm they seem in the traffic,
as if resting on a river bank
or by a paddy field,
watching the clouds.

In the Streets of Jakarta 2

They just woke up,
huddled together on a mat,
protected by small trees
growing in the centre
of a busy roundabout.

And now they stand,
shovel gripped in their hands,
shirts and trousers
almost the colour
of the soil they move.

Do they just stand?
Oh no, they stretch and jump,
hair flying,
dark eyes shining,
and they laugh!

Soon they'll set out
for some rice and a mug of tea,
then start digging.
Happy they are
to have work and a bed.

Hosanna's Poems

Hosanna (Emily) Kingston, age 77, is the latest newcomer to the Poetry Group. With a profound Christian faith, she is also a Subud member.

The following spiritual and beautiful poems were written before she came to us, and we are proud to present them as part of the first Wisma Mulia collection.

OUR DANCE

Written for 'DRUM' disabled art group, March 2007

Life is a dance, a dance of love,
gentle it comes, as the wings of a dove.

If you can't wave your arms and your legs won't start,
play with the paint and dance with your heart.

Blue chases red, purple flowers appear,
yellow meets blue and green leaves are there.

Lines interact, they spring up and down,
circles swirl around and squares squat down.

Hold hands with your brush and show it the way,
put on some music and let's dance all day.

CRADLE SONG

Cradling me
Rocking me
Loving me
Caress of love
Wings of the dove.
Take my care
Take my sorrow
Take my fear.
Wash me clean
Raise me high
Teach me, Lord,
To fly with Thee.
Then back to earth
To live in Thee,
Rooted, grounded,
In the tree.
The tree of life
Sheltering me,
So let it be.

SPRING

Like brooms the bare trees gently sweep the sky

Revealing light in blue and green and white.

Then buds create a haze of gold on green and mauve.

How come? When on the earth men maim and kill

And flowers push up to perish in the storm.

The landscape of the sky retains

Its power to celebrate eternal light.

Then, even when dark falls, the birds

Sing out their knowledge of the Spring

And we, in Easter Praise, cry out -

Jesus is here and lives with us tonight.

TWO LOVE POEMS

I

All, oh Lord, I give to Thee
Then so beautifully
You carry me, cradled in your arms
You call to me, that the face I see
Is also hidden deep in me.
I drink from the cup
Then the cup is in me
Holding me, holding me.
Carry me, Father, over the sea,
Always there to rest with Thee.
Love in my heart, Love in my hands,
This is the dance I understand.
Show me, dear Lord, how to be
Always, always close to Thee.

II

Love it is the meaning, Love it is the way,
And you're loving us every single day
The soul it is a blossom, the soul it is a flower,
And your grace waters us, every single hour.
Love it is a mountain, Love it is a dream,
And it carries us like a living stream.
Love it is a rainbow, Love it is a star,
As you gently lead us to a world afar.
Love it is the meaning,
Love it is the way,
So let's hold hands together
And celebrate today . . .

CHANGE

Christ the anchor of my being

Radiance too bright for seeing

As I dangle in the void and swing

I know your love doth hold me fast.

And one day your golden string

Will very gently pull me in,

There to rest in calm above,

Home at last, in Father's love.

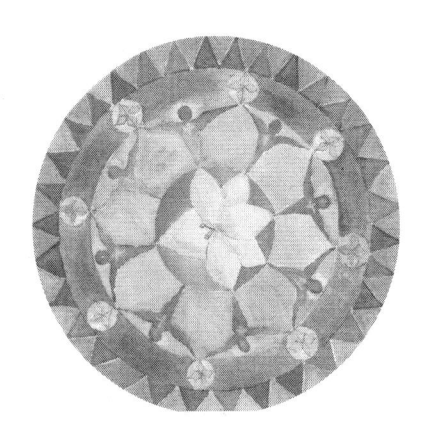

A Word About Mandalas

MANDALA is a Sanskrit word. In the Buddhist and Hindu religious traditions their sacred art often takes a mandala form. The basic form is a square with four gates containing a circle with a centre point. These concentric diagrams have a spiritual and a ritual significance.

A mandala can be used for focusing attention, as a spiritual teaching tool, for establishing a sacred space, and as an aid to meditation. Its symbolic nature can help us access deep levels of the unconscious, and allow the meditator to experience a 'mystical sense of oneness with the ultimate unity from which the cosmos in all its manifold forms arises.' (*David Fontana, Psychologist*).

Forms that are evocative of mandalas are prevalent in Christianity: the Celtic Cross, the aureole, rose windows, and so forth. Tibetan monks frequently make very beautiful temporary mandalas from coloured sands.

Hosanna has long enjoyed painting mandalas herself. Here is her explanation, written in December 2011.

HOMAGE TO THE CIRCLE

A circle is a wondrous thing,
It warms us with the shining sun,
Sends us the magic of full moon.
Globe-like we know our world is round
And although we are spread around
Our lives are joined, the world is one.

In a circle gently sharing
Words, falling in a pool of silence,
Echo round like pebbles stirring.
Hearts are touched and healing flows
From a greater heart above
Holding each one in His love.

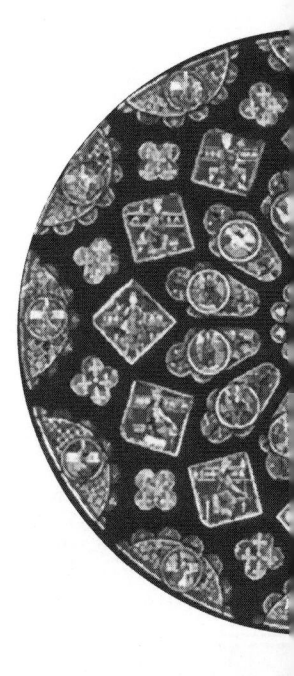

In a circle we can dance, we can sing,
Weaving, with gifts of touch and sound,
A pattern greater than our own.
Song flying up into the sky
Feet strumming down into the ground.
May the angels join our sound.

Mandalas are what I love to paint
The circle is my holding space,
More welcoming than the empty page
With memories of essays and school days.
Here I am free to splash and play
To celebrate God's world each day.

But best of all the blessing is,
For each of us the circle is,
The symbol of our coming home,
The wonder of God's will being done,
His love fulfilled in everyone.

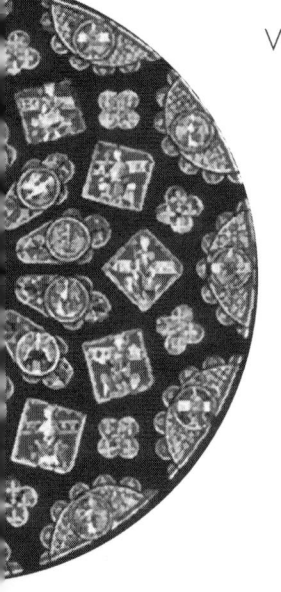

Monica's Poems

Monica, for many years a lecturer in English at the University of the West of England and elsewhere, responded somewhat diffidently when I asked if she had any previously-written poems she would like to contribute to our book. Finally, she modestly presented me with the following small collection, passing them off as inconsequential. However, the quality of the writing is at once apparent. Monica is a poet of no small talent.

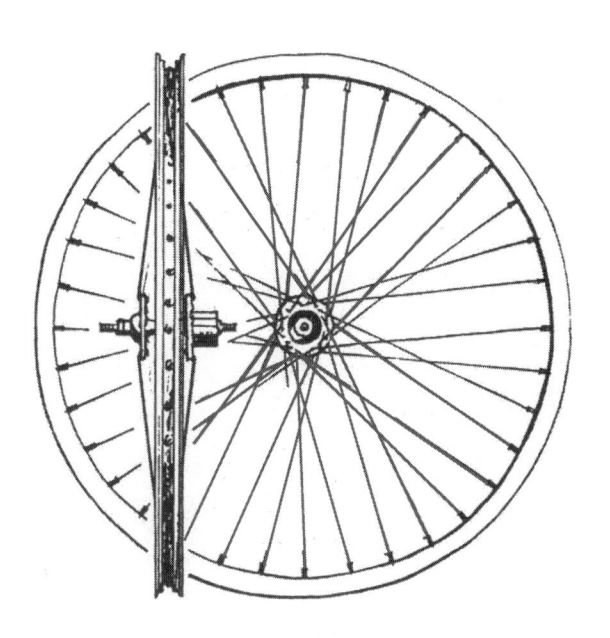

For a Departed Cyclist

As you go your way,
May no hurtling vehicle brush you,
No sudden door swing open,
No driver's curse follow.

May your wheel go spinning in a freewheel headlong
And the hills be kind.
Let the wind gather and speed you,
Like your father teaching you to ride when you were small.

May your brakes be sound and your saddle firm.
May no shards lie in wait for you –
All cycle lanes be taxi free.

Let boughs sway where you ride,
The sun be a mild bath, and the rain cool you.

May your paths lead where, in the glide of water
For ever
Giant beeches gaze.

The End of History

"Millennium," they promised. "A new start.
Expand the heart – open the mind.
Let's watch the generals and their troops depart,
We'll learn to count the alien as a friend."

While civic stars in town squares showered and sputtered
And strangers hugged in public – even then
A cynical small demon in you muttered,
"We'll be at one another's throats tomorrow noon."

Not knowing, then, the towers that would topple,
The mountains burst apart by freedom's bombs
In lands where few could pinpoint the Big Apple
On maps they never owned. Shattered homes

And shattered bodies. So the Empire wins:
This lousy war is done. A new begins.

Fashion

You have your acolytes. Slave devotees.
(Should I be faithful also? Have I been?)
No wonder your first syllable agrees
With lash. But jackboots aren't at all my scene –

They hobble-pinch your ankles, crush your toe –
Or sweatshops, hothouses, or orchids, either.
Considering lilies always moved me, though,
And walking naked enterprise – no bother.

Whether garbed, kitted out, attired, or clad at all,
What, honestly, does it matter? What may fold
A comforter round creeping age seems best.
No Logo's guaranteed against the cold.

Take it from me, then, step out smartly dressed
By Serendipity of Oxfam. (Cool!)

The City Speaks

When the space below Park Street
Was a thicket of masts
And urchins mudlarked among the carriages
My cellars sheltered an African child.
He rocked himself to sleep,
Cheeks wet with the shipwreck of home.

On my ledges, feather-fluffed,
Pigeons huddle. In doorways
Sleepers cough.
In the slicing March wind, a green script unfurls on branches.

I've seen kindness and abuse, like all cities –
Slow violence visited on wage slaves,
Epiphanies of sharing.

Down centuries, I've watched the swapping
Of votes, banknotes, drugs and weapons,
Of plots of land (where today, under dapple of boughs
The picnic rugs are spread) –
Seats, backhanders, winks and promises –

Watched grey stone and red, and glass
Rear, shatter and crumble by the river.
In the menace of sky-borne engines
Terraces folded in flame.

My foundations burrow in Saxon clay,
My roots tangle in the mud of Avon.
Married to rivers, I give birth to the Atlantic.

From Brandon Hill – where today
Driven leaves are golden swarms –
I've followed my children, hope and regret in their breasts,
Swept out under spread sails, or in the clasp of Brunel's
iron lady,
On a westward-flowing tide, to bless and plunder.

On nights when panes are virgin frost fields,
Or streaming with rain
My rooms have cradled a million nativities,
Lamps of a thousand Diwalis, Ramadans.

You move away from me, but never forget,
As you swoop towards me, returning out of the darkness,
In a myriad points of orange light I cry to you,
Home! Home.

My Verse is Bright Green, and Blazing Crimson

Hardly the subtlety of light
Waning on wet sand.

From depths of summer,
No obscured bird's call.

No shifting-evanescent
Rainbow in oil.

No tangled bindweed
Knot of twisted strands.

Anticipate, rather,
A swoop of wave over rock –
Clamour of gulls, a gust of wind –

A flinging wide of arms –
A shout of sunrise –

Switchback of a hillside under
Slowly pyrotechnic trees –

A brave rag flourished at a distance.

Night Noises

What are those footsteps on the stairs? Bears?
My neck hair bristles. I clench my toes.
What's that noise like a muffled growl?
A hunting beast on a jungle prowl?
No – only Aunt Ruby blowing her nose.
But what's that humming? What's that squeaking?
A hiss like a snake – then people speaking?
Just the water pipes. And the roof beams creaking.
But what's that music whispering low?
There's a room that's haunted in the flat below!
It's only the neighbour's radio.
What's that light from behind the stars?
An alien ship coming down from Mars?
Just the moon, slanting down behind some jars.
You only heard the window rattle,
A vixen scream, a dead leaf scuttle –
Whatever the reason, it'll keep.

Now turn right over, and go to sleep.

The Quest

No sign of Africa yet –
No blinding mooncurve of sand
No foam breaking on rocks
No tree branch bobbing.

For days,
Unquiet waters roll under
As they veer and steady
With relentless telepathic instinct
Southward and southward.

Seen high against the fading light they are
A swarm of flies
Milling with directed purpose.
The rigging of a passing ship a haven
The lighthouse tower blaze a trap.

Pane broken bodies
Engulfed in swell
Vanish.
Scimitar wings ice-pinioned
Numb with beating
To left and right, drop. Still
The flock with unanimous contact

In an ocean of twittering cries
In a reddening sky
Travels. The tiny bodies thrust on
Dying, singing.

The Aid Worker

Lull fear asleep, and let your spirit show,
You hope to save one life before you die –
Give me one sign of love before you go.

Reaping a hurricane that others sow,
You'll walk with empty hands where killers lie.
Lull fear asleep, and let your spirit show.

We'll stand some day where quiet waters flow.
Now, rush to the scene. You hardly question why –
Give me one sign of love before you go.

Prepared to lose you many lives ago,
Would I prefer you wring your hands and cry?
Lull fear asleep, and let your spirit show.

I think you'd have me sit at home and sew,
If you can look our children in the eye –
Give me one sign of love before you go.

The life you save may be the life you know –
Treading your way beneath a lowering sky,
Lull fear asleep and let your spirit show –
Give me one sign of love before you go.

Leaving the Ceilidh

The grown-ups whoop and giggle and bump,
Free to let go. Sticking it out to the end.

Mistress of the maze, the tiniest child
Skips seriously,
Re-tracing the patterns – Dozy Do – Grand Star –

Again and again.
"Link your arms and swing your partner –
Swing your partner One two three."

Revolving on one another's hands,
A tubby, greying couple.
In the tender recognition of thirty years
Time holds its breath.

Top couple down the centre
Others follow.
Richard and Rachel
Horse it with flapping hair.

Now – big circle!
All the dancers
Kicking up their heels. Swirling round
And round. Panting. Faces alight.

Stand in the darkened passage,
Watching unseen
Your friends, laughing without you –

Feeling blessed to recognise, when you have to leave,
Whether they think of you a bit, or never at all,

Behind you
The dance goes on.

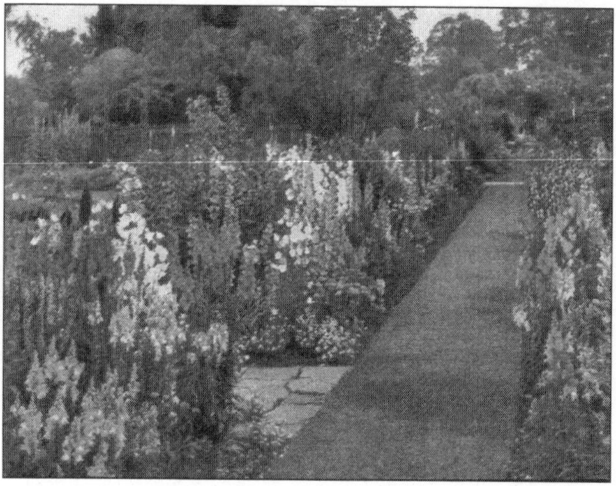

The beautiful front aspect of Wisma's main house, with the garden room and wing of apartments just visible to the left.

Ground floor passageway to the apartments, with a feel of the Mediterranean.

Some of the group members. From left to right: *Nancy, Patricia (foreground), Maryse, Aine, Naomi, Steph (foreground), Fiona, Iris.*

Some of the Wisma Mulia staff members. Back: *Hassan (Maintenance), Penny (Chef), Pauline (Carer), Lyn (Driver), Carole (Domestic), Lindsay (Carer), Gregory (Actor – visiting!)* Front: *Dawn (Secretary), Steph (Author), Philip (Manager), Cheryl (Carer), Joyce (Laundry).*

Patricia and Steph caught unawares.

Aine.

Fiona.

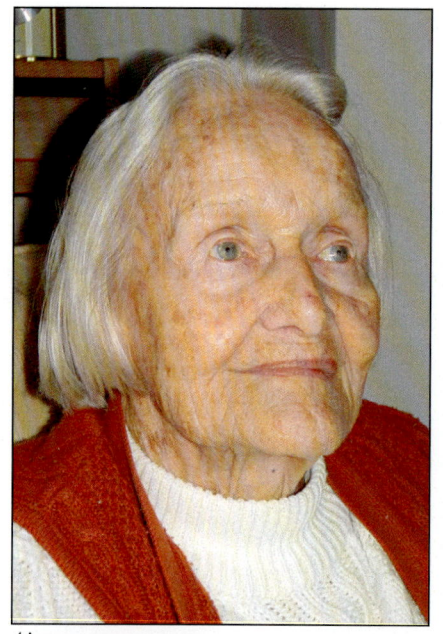

Iris.

Maryse.

Naomi.

Patricia wearing her fascinator.

Nancy.

Steph working on her tan in Thailand.

Wisma Mulia Garden Party. Top left: *Fiona enjoying the afternoon's events.*
Top right: *Jim searching for someone.* Middle left: *Iris enjoys an ice cream.*
Bottom: *The late Leila seated with Aine and Maryse.*

Maryse after another colourful scarf.

Monica using her sales skills.

Philip with Maryse.

Philip gets the wet sponge treatment.

Mandalas painted by Hosanna in watercolour. (See page 99).

Chapter 7

Interviews with Group Members

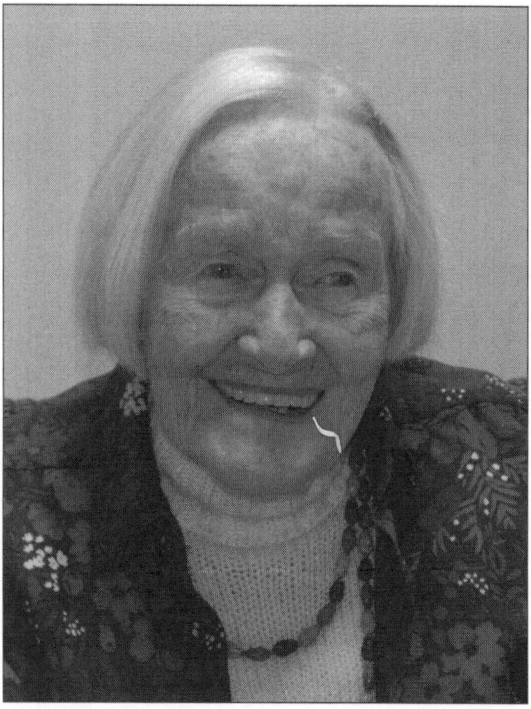

Interview – Aine

Aine: I am Aine Branting. My first name was Helga, and I was always called Helga until I received my Subud name, Aine. I was born on 24th December 1914, the first year of the First World War.
Steph: You've seen a lot in your life.
Aine: I certainly have. I was born and brought up in Berlin.
Steph: How long did you live there?
Aine: I got married in 1938, and my husband was given permission to finish his studies as a teacher. So our family moved away from Berlin to Frankfurt on the Oder. Our daughter was born nine months after we got married and we called her Elke Maria. (She later received the Subud name Melinda.) My husband never finished his studies. He was called up for military service and sent into Poland, where he was killed.
Steph: That must have been a terrible time for you.
Aine: It was amazing how much strength I was given. I had a lot of support from my husband after he died.
Steph: *After* he died. Ah, I understand . . . Did you expect that?
Aine: Yes, I had, actually – it's difficult to explain. One afternoon I put my daughter in the cot for her afternoon sleep as usual. This was in the summer of 1941. I bent over to kiss her,

and suddenly I had this horrendous pain digging into my back, like . . . tearing it, tearing it up. It was a *terrific* pain. And she was lying there with her hands up, looking at me, absolutely still. She was part of this experience. And I knew it was my husband. Two or three weeks later I got a letter from the Army.
Steph: But you already knew.
Aine: When the postman came I looked at him and said, 'Oh, yes,' and he stared at me. Melinda was crawling all over the place by then saying 'Da-da-da-da'. She had loved it so much to have her dad at home. My family and friends in Berlin rallied round and sent me messages saying, you must come back to Berlin, we don't want you to stay there in that little village for the rest of your life. So I did. In the Autumn of 1941 we moved back in with my mother. I decided to finish my music studies at the Academy for School and Church Music. It was situated in a beautiful park, in an old little castle. It was a wonderful place with marvellous teachers. I had a lovely time studying violin and piano for one year. Of course, my father was a pianist, my mother a concert singer.
Steph: I remember you telling us when we read D.H. Lawrence's poem 'Piano' at the group that it brought back memories of when you used to sit under the piano at home when your father was playing.
Aine: Grand piano! Yes. My mother would be singing, and I saw their legs.
Steph: Side by side. That's a lovely image. So what did you do when you finished your studies?
Aine: I got a job. I wanted us to get out of Berlin, and there was

a lovely school – they had schools for the Hitler Youth Leaders all over the country. So I got this job, not far from the East border of Germany in a very beautiful, mountainous area. As time passed, the school had to move several times because the Russians were making threatening noises, and we ended up in the centre of Germany, half way between Stuttgart and Munich.

We had a brilliant High School teacher, a sports teacher, a language teacher, and me. We stayed there until the end of the war, when we got the message from Berlin that we should leave at midnight on Easter Monday of 1945, and make our way to Ulm. So we packed a suitcase each. I had a little pushcart. As well as the four of us and Elke there were some girls from the Hitler Youth who had been helping round the house, cooking, washing and all that, who came with us. We left on tip-toe and went into the forest, going south.

Steph: Dramatic.

Aine: Oh, very dramatic. We had been very secluded. We weren't allowed to listen to any radio other than the official statements, so we didn't know what was going on. And then we started to meet groups of soldiers in tattered uniforms saying, 'The war's finished. We're going home.' And we suddenly realised what was happening.

Steph: Where did you end up?

Aine: We decided to stay together as far as Ulm, which was a government administration centre. There we were given a spot on the cold floor to sleep, some food, and our final salary. Then we all said goodbye at a big crossroads, and everyone went their own way to find their family.

I had the address of my mother-in-law, who lived with her daughter, Inge. She had a baby daughter two years younger than Melinda. They all lived south of Munich in the foothills of the Alps.

We stayed there for a while and then one day I had a visitor. It was Nelda, the leader of the school. She had found her mother and one of her sisters in Breslau. They survived the horrendous air attacks they had there. That city was smashed to pieces. By then Germany was divided, west from east. Nelda had brought her mother and sister out of the east zone. She was a genius, a very clever woman, very skilled in many ways. She was a great artist and she made beautiful dolls' heads. She and her mother and sister had set up a little business making dolls, because you couldn't get any toys in those days. And they sold well, particularly on the big farms all around that area. They bartered them for butter and cheese and managed very well.

Nelda asked me if I would like to join her and become part of this enterprise. I thought it was a marvellous idea. My little daughter was also very ready to get away from Oma's family. It was a good decision for all of us.

Steph: Time to go.
Aine: Time to go. But we stayed in the south. The north had been badly bombed, there was no food, and everything was in total chaos.
Steph: How long did you continue with Nelda in the doll-making business?
Aine: Until the currency changed from the Rentenmark to the Deutschmark. All banks were closed for two days while the

change was made, and everybody was given 10 DM to keep going on. Yes, everyone in the whole country started off with 10 DM. But, do you know, within two days there were already rich and poor? It was amazing. Some people had stored so much stuff. When this new currency came out, suddenly all the shops were full of this stuff! People with only 10 DM couldn't do much shopping. They just had to start from scratch.

Steph: So what did you do next?

Aine: Well, Nelda got back into the teaching profession. I just found myself a job in a local oil company as a secretary – I'd trained as a secretary in 1933 when my father died, because my mother was then on her own with my brother and sisters, one of them still a baby. So now I got this job with a company that produced every kind of oil, from crude oil through to the very finest machine oil for weaving machines. It was quite interesting, quite demanding, and, of course, I had to learn a lot of new things. But the boss was a marvellous man. The company owned a lot of property in that little town, and we were given a very nice ground floor flat with a garden.

When Elke finished primary school, I enrolled her at a Rudolf Steiner School, beautifully situated in the next valley. She was very happy there. Then, out of the blue, I got a letter from Australia. I had had no contact with Australia, although my mother was born there and my father grew up on a Mission Station north of Adelaide.

Steph: So you'd had quite a solid religious upbringing.

Aine: Well, no. Because father was sent to Germany to study to become an architect. Being so far away from his family, he decided they wouldn't know what he was doing, so he studied music instead, and became a professional pianist and music teacher. And that's how he met my mother, who had a beautiful soprano voice. They gave lots of concerts in Berlin and, during the war, for the soldiers.

Steph: What about religion in your childhood home?

Aine: My father had decided to break his relationship with the church when he came to Germany. So I had no formal religious education until I went to school. We had a wonderful religious teacher, marvellous. I think I'm still very much based in what she taught me.

Steph: You were Protestant?

Aine: Yes.

Steph: And you suddenly got a letter from Australia.

Aine: Out of the blue. From somebody I'd never heard of. And this lady told me that they'd found a letter in their attic after nearly 30 years. My mother died before the end of the war. She caught a bad case of 'flu. It was a terrible epidemic. I was not quite four. I remember very well my father taking me into this room and saying, 'You have to say goodbye to your Mummy. She has to leave you.' She was already dead then; it was the day of the funeral. And this lady in Australia had just found a letter from my father, written after my mother died, asking them to look after me if anything should happen to him.

Steph: And who was she?

Aine: They were a young couple who had been very great friends with my parents in the early days in Melbourne. But they'd lost the letter. When they discovered it, thirty years later, they got onto the Red Cross in Germany and gave them my name, Helga Wendlandt, and they found me. I didn't know these people existed. So then we started writing to each other, and she told me I had an Aunt, a sister of my mother, living in Australia. It was all completely new to me. Within two years I'd decided to emigrate to Australia, taking my daughter with me. It was 1956 and it looked as if there would be another war, between Russia and America. I thought, I've got to get her out of here. So I wrote to them and told them how I felt, and they wanted us to come over anyway. So Aunty Hilda and Uncle Ted got in touch with an Italian shipping company and booked us on a ship to Melbourne.

Steph: Had you learned English at school?

Aine: Oh, yes. And my parents spoke English all the time between themselves. I grew up bilingual. And then, of course, I took lessons in English shorthand, because I was fluent in German shorthand, and I took another secretarial job. Bosch at that time had a large company in Melbourne, supplying all the fuel injection equipment for Mercedes and Volkswagen.

Steph: Did you enjoy life in Melbourne?

Aine: Oh, yes. For me, it was like coming home. Both my grandmothers had sent us Christmas parcels from Australia, and the fragrance of eucalyptus from the wrappings used to make me feel quite homesick, even though I'd never been there!

Steph: Is that where you met Maryse?

Aine: Yes. She lived in Melbourne.

Steph: And is that where you became Subud?

Aine: Yes. I would never have found Subud if I'd stayed in that small town in Germany. It's not very big there.

Steph: So it was meant to be, your going to Australia.

Aine: Absolutely, absolutely! Maryse and I met at Subud gatherings. In the meantime, I met and married my second husband, Laurence, who comes from Sweden. He was brought up on a big farm there, the youngest of twelve children. He had been a diesel engineer on a ship when he met his first wife, and they had travelled in America and India and had an exciting time. Then they settled in Sydney. Gurdjieff* had an active group there and they attended the meetings. There was to be a world gathering in England at Coombe Springs, and Laurence decided to go. While he was there, his wife became very ill and died. Bapak* had come to England for the first time, and he met Laurence who was very upset and sad. Bapak advised him to go to Melbourne, where he would find his second wife.

Steph: And it was you!

Aine: And it was me. We had a very loving marriage. And we were very active in Subud.

Steph: And you went to Indonesia!

Aine: Yes, we first went just for four weeks, for a visit. Eventually we lived in Indonesia for twenty years. I loved it there.

Steph: How did you come to be living at Wisma Mulia, Aine?

Aine: Well, I'd known about it for many years. After my divorce I came to live in England because my daughter had settled here with her family, and I moved into Wisma six years ago, after my daughter died from cancer.

*Gurdjieff; *Bapak; see page 192.

Steph: And how has it been for you?
Aine: It's been lovely, absolutely lovely. It's the only Subud Home for the elderly in the world, which I really don't understand, as Subud is in about 70 countries now.
Steph: It seems to me that Subud people are very particular people, very positive people.
Aine: Yes. And they try to live in this world according to the will of God, as true 'human' beings.
Steph: You've seen some of your friends die here. This is a very personal question and you may elect not to answer it: what do you feel when you think of your own death?
Aine: Anticipation.
Steph: That sounds almost joyous. You're in a good place here and now, but you can look forward with equanimity and move towards your end?
Aine: 'End' is perhaps the wrong word. I would say 'departure'.
Steph: You've had an amazing life, haven't you!
Aine: (laughing) Some would say so.
Steph: You may not remember, but I wonder what you thought when I arrived here and said there was to be a poetry group?
Aine: I don't remember the beginning, but it's all been very stimulating. I think I've learned a lot. I've lived with poetry for many years, on and off. I wouldn't have continued to come if it hadn't given me so much pleasure. And I've enjoyed this interview too. Thank you.

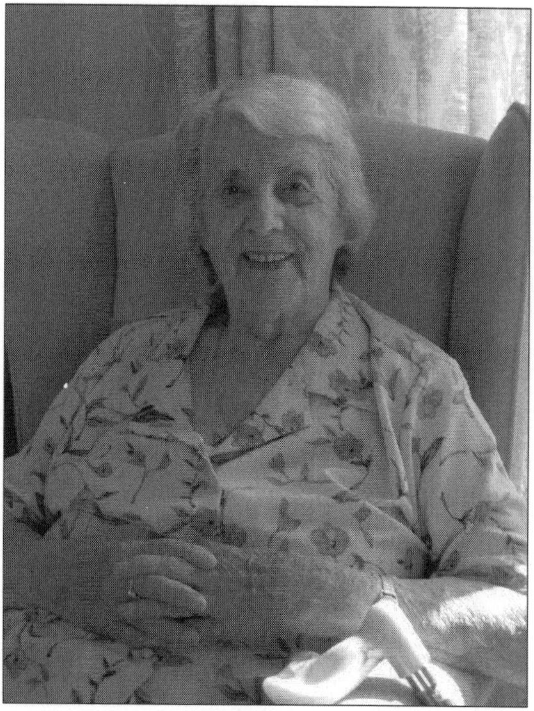

Interview – Iris

Steph: Tell me your name and date of birth, Iris.
Iris: Elsie Swain, 19th January, 1917. I was born in the northeast of England.
Steph: Don't you share a birthday with Patricia? Isn't she January 19th as well?
Iris: Yes, but she's seven years younger than me.
Steph: So you're an amazing 96. Tell me something about yourself.
Iris: Before my marriage I was just living at home with my family. I was fairly fortunate – my father had bought a car and a boat. We used to go upriver in the boat. I had very strict parents. I wasn't allowed to go just anywhere, I had to say where I was going. And I wasn't allowed to talk to boys. I had a friend who kept me on the straight and narrow.
Steph: You were married quite young, weren't you?
Iris: Yes, I met my first husband when I was seventeen. He was the local doctor's son. The war came, and he still hadn't finished his exams at that time. (Later he qualified as an accountant.) I went to live in his father the doctor's house. In wartime people do strange things. My husband went abroad with the Air Force, and I went to be a hairdresser for the

French Lycée in the Lake District. One of our children was born in wartime. My husband looked ever so sheepish when he came back from the war and I handed him an eighteen-month-old baby! I had another girl, my second child, Penny, in 1946.

Steph: And how did you meet your second husband?

Iris: After our marriage ended in a divorce I wasn't going to get married again. But then I went on a cruise. The cruise director was very handsome. When he started dancing with the unattached guests, the first one was me. All the tours we went on, he went with me. Five weeks after the cruise was ended, I married him. We were so happy.

Steph: And you changed your name. You changed your name twice.

Iris: Yes. I had hairdressing salons, one of them in Majorca. And Elsie's not a very attractive name. So I changed it and called my salon Suzi – S-U-Z-I.

Steph: Very chic.

Iris: I was Suzi for quite a while. I wasn't called Elsie until I came here, and then I got a bit tired of it. In Subud, you know, it's quite in order to change your name. It's quite an occasion.

Steph: Why is that?

Iris: I don't know the reason why, but other people have done it. Aine did it. And we had ever so many people. Goodness knows where they all came from. We don't normally have so many, a big circle like that. I can't remember the first name I decided on. And they all shut their eyes for a few minutes and then they all said, 'Nooo!' So I had to think again, so then I thought . . . Are you interested in Subud? Do you know anything about it?

Steph: A little bit, yes.

Iris: Anyway, I said 'Iris' – it was all very pleasant, you know. All this was in the Latihan* Hall.

Steph: And it was a naming ceremony?

Iris: Yes. And there were people who don't live here, you know, all from Subud. So they all said, 'Yes, yes!' to Iris. It was amazing.

Steph: And how was it that you first got involved with Subud?

Iris: Yes, well, my husband had Alzheimer's. I nursed him for seven years. And then I couldn't manage any more and he went into a home up north. But that home was sold and my daughter told me about another one near here and I had him moved there. I didn't want to stay in our house on my own, so my daughter and I looked around and we found Wisma. And my husband was nearby, just at the other end of the village. I could visit him on my electric scooter. Philip hadn't been here very long when I came, only a week or two. You know what he is, full of charm. He wasn't as cuddly then as he is now! Anyway, I'd never heard of Subud then.

Steph: And when you came here you began to hear about it?

Iris: Yes. I was friends with a Dutch lady here, Virginia, quite a talented artist. I used to cook for her – I was livelier then – I used to make cakes and things because she was nearly blind. She was a Subud. But she didn't talk about it. It wasn't until I got really friendly with her that I found out what went on behind that door to the Latihan Hall. She asked me if I'd ever thought of joining, and she got me interested.

* Latihan. See page 192.

Steph: And have you appreciated being a member?
Iris: Oh, yes. Also, you can be whatever religion and be a Subud. I'm a Spiritualist, really. I did a lot of healing at one time.
Steph: Really?
Iris: Yes. I don't do it now because you've got to be fit. As well as making someone better, you could, equally, pass on something to make them feel unwell.
Steph: So you'd been here at least four years by the time I arrived. I'm wondering what you thought to yourself when you heard there was going to be a Poetry Group.
Iris: Oh, well, I'm the sort of person who's always interested in things, you know? Life's a bit boring if you don't have something to think about.
Steph: Well, I seem to remember you saying, 'Oh, I'm not coming to that – I hate poetry!'
Iris: Did I?
Steph: Yes, you did.
Iris: Well, it's true. I *wasn't* particularly interested in poetry.
Steph: And now how do you feel on a Friday morning when you know there's going to be a poetry group meeting?
Iris: I hope I've got the right day! And I look forward to it because it's pleasant, and it's friendly, and it's OK. I did hate poetry at school. It all depends on who you are and how you're made. There were girls at school who could read something through three times and they had it off. Not me, oh no! It was hard for me, not something I enjoyed.
Steph: So, were you surprised when you found yourself enjoying it?

Iris: Yes, well that's because there are personalities. At school you're just sat behind a desk . . . Now I find I'm there waiting for you to come back again before you've even gone!

Steph: (laughing) And what about the reading aloud?

Iris: Yes, it's nice.

Steph: I've told you that you read very well, haven't I?

Iris: Well, I try to put something into it!

Steph: You certainly do. You're very expressive, very well-paced.

Iris: Yes, it's all very stimulating. And you manage to drag a lot out of all of us. I think the book will be special – it's got to be. While you're away, I'll be saying, 'When *is* she coming back?'

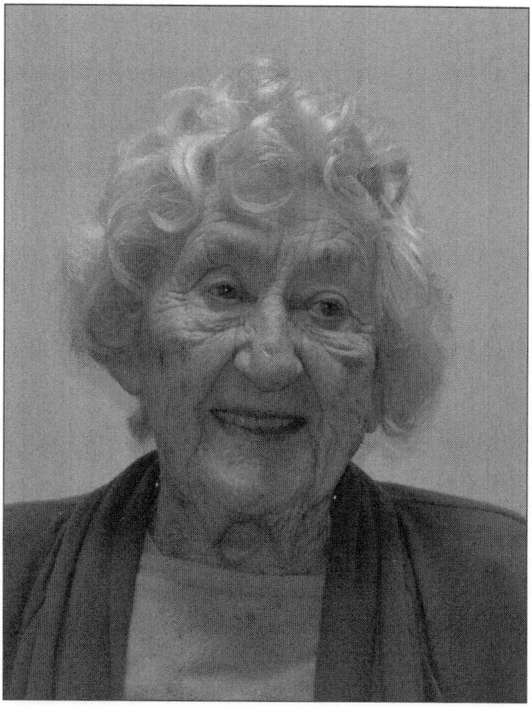

Interview – Patricia

Steph: Are you used to having your voice recorded, Patricia?
Patricia: I've had it done a couple of times – interviews, I mean.
Steph: Good. Now, tell me your full name and date of birth.
Patricia: Crikey! My name is Patricia Pamela Garland Hewitson/Lacey.
Steph: Wow! What a handle!
Patricia: Well, you asked for it. Lacey was at the end when I got married.
Steph: And your date of birth?
Patricia: 19th January 1923.
Steph: And that makes you how old now?
Patricia: That's a good question, isn't it. 88.
Steph: Phenomenal!
Patricia: Is it? Some of the ladies are over 90.
Steph: Yes, but you're catching up fast, aren't you! (Patricia laughs) Would you tell me a bit about your life?
Patricia: I was brought up in a small village in the north of England. The village was my playground. At age twelve I discovered the music on the radio, opera, I mean. My ears were pierced to the opera from then on. I remember my first time to the opera, when I was about 15. I was very excited.

We were spending two months in London with a rich uncle. He had a chauffeur who took us everywhere in a Rolls! Mother did take me for an audition at Guildhall School of Music in London later because of my singing voice, but Father couldn't afford to pay for me there. But I was often asked to open local bazaars and village activities.

Steph: Because of your voice?

Patricia: Yes. I was a soprano. I'd sing an aria from *Traviata* or *Carmen*, or something. But I got most of my education from Lawrence Olivier!

Steph: How was that?

Patricia: I was always at the theatre – Leicester Square, the New Theatre, the Old Vic. I used to pay to sit up in the Gods, and then look out for an empty seat in the stalls or the dress circle. I could usually move to a better seat. I saw Olivier in *The Entertainer*. Do you know that? I was at the front of the stalls. There was Larry, tap-dancing! I began to have hysterics – everyone was looking at me. He began to look at, respond to me. In the end the whole dance was for me. I wrote to him about it afterwards, and I got back a two-page letter handwritten by him, saying that it had made him very happy to read that he had such an impact on people's lives.

Steph: It sounds as if you had an exciting time!

Patricia: It was fun. I used to run an old A35 van, you know, not with windows in the sides, it was closed in. Once, I'd been to a performance at Glyndebourne and I didn't want to go home in full evening dress. I stood at the front and the man drove my van round to me, alongside all the Rolls Royces. I changed in the van and put on a tennis dress with a jersey on top.

Steph: I wondered if you could tell me how you came to be living at Wisma.

Patricia: That's a memory to think. Well, do you know the history of Wisma starting? When it first started, I was a trained nurse and a nursery school teacher, so I had two different kinds of training. And so I came here to help get Wisma off the ground. I lived here for two or three months.

Steph: What was your role, then? What were you doing in that process?

Patricia: I was a Manager of some kind, working under the jurisdiction of David and Emma.

Steph: So were you one of the first people to see residents come into the building?

Patricia: Yes. It was a bit of a jump from one age to another, because I'd run nursery schools before that.

Steph: When did you first start doing jobs in the caring profession?

Patricia: Well, I began when I was three-and-a-half years of age, in the village we lived in. I loved children so much that I went to every household in the village that had a newborn baby and took them their first present, and from when I was about four, I was always the first person to go with the mother to wheel the baby out. My sister said, 'You'd go through the village and suddenly you'd see this big pram with nobody behind it, and the mother about ten yards behind.' And who was pushing the pram but little old me! So I've loved babies from the time I was born.

When I was nearly thirty I'd only had one ectopic pregnancy

and very nearly died, so we gave up the idea of having any children. Instead of that, when I came back to England from South Africa I was asked to start the first nursery school in South Highgate. After two years I felt I wanted something wider. These were the days when there weren't any immigrants; the first to come were the West Indians in 1951, then the Pakistanis came in, then the Bangladeshis.

I had a dream. I dreamed I was sitting on a haystack with all the colours in the world – Africans, Indians, Chinese, English, everything, sitting on this haystack. In the dream the man said, 'Now receive what you must do.' I thought, 'What the hell does that mean?' And I asked Bapak if he could tell me. He said, 'No, you will find out yourself, you will understand your dream if you wait.'

And a month later someone rang me up from the Council and said, 'Patricia, you've been recommended to start the first multi-ethnic nursery school, now all the immigrants are coming in. And, if it's successful, would you start more?' I did that for the next fifteen years. I had a very, very good staff. Two of them who eventually took over from me started with me as young children of eighteen.

Steph: How many nursery schools were there?
Patricia: I started them in West Hampstead and Kilburn – I started seven or eight.
Steph: And are they still running now?
Patricia: One or two of them are. They're full-day nurseries now. It was quite a while before we took on really young children. We didn't really approve of it in the early days. We thought mothers

should keep their children at home until they were four.

Steph: Why did you decide to move here as a resident, then?

Patricia: Because I belonged to the Subud movement, and I often came here and ran it because I was well-trained. I used to take over from Sparkes and his wife, who used to run it then, when they needed a holiday. And I think I filled in for a number of staff.

Steph: Can you tell me how you found Subud, Patricia?

Patricia: I think one of the things Bapak said was, 'We don't find it, God finds us'. My parents were very religious, but I was an atheist. My mother took me into Westminster Abbey when I was fifteen, and I swore never to go into a church again until I'd found out what all the rubbish about God was about.

So I never did, and then the Gurdjieff work started, as you know – I was now twenty-eight – and my husband, who came from South Africa, said, 'I'm going to take you to some lectures on this philosopher called Gurdjieff.' And he told me a bit about the meaning of it all. I said, 'Good God, you'll be taking me into a church next!' He said, 'If you and I ever find God and go to church together we'll be very lucky people.'

We attended Gurdjieff classes at Coombe Springs for two years before Subud came in 1955. In 1957 we met Bapak, and I looked after Bapak's wife, Ibu. I arranged for the housekeeping to be done in shifts, and I always took the early shift, from 6.00 in the morning to 2.00 in the afternoon. On the way to the house I would often get an inner indication to get a melon or a grapefruit, and would pick them up en route from the shops that would open very early in the immigrant neighbourhoods. And as soon as I arrived at the house, the person caring for Ibu would come out and say, 'Patricia, Ibu wants such-and-such' – and that was always the thing I'd already picked up. That was such a blessing, to make her comfortable and to give her things that she loved.

And then she sent for me one day. She said, 'Tell Patricia I want her.' So I went in – it was in the afternoon – and she said, 'Just sit, Patricia.' So I sat by her side and she said, 'Now receive.' And so I went off into space with Ibu there, I went off on a big journey, I think about ten minutes. And then she said, 'Yah, that's it, Patricia.' And then she said, 'Ibu wants to tell you how happy you've made her.'

When I first met Bapak I was frightened to death of him – I wanted to keep at least fifty yards away from him. It took me ten or fifteen years before I could sit close to him. He used to laugh and wave his hand. He used to call, 'Patricia,' and laugh. I didn't want to show my dirty self to him. He could see right through you, he knew everything. I was too ashamed. I'd only just come into Subud. I had lots to get rid of.

Steph: And, now you're at Wisma, how is it?

Patricia: For me? Oh, I love it. And my sister came here also, as you know. She was five or six years older than me. She didn't want to come at first, but when she did, we had a great life here, she and I. We were free, and we just had enough money to run a car. So we often used to go out to lunch at the local restaurants. The staff absolutely adored Margaret. Of the two of us, she was the one most like my mother. She had a very sweet, kind temperament.

Steph: So Margaret died here, then?

Patricia: Yes, she did. And the staff threw themselves on the bed and cried, three of them. That's how well-loved she was. They don't do that for everyone.
Steph: No, I'm sure they don't. Now, Patricia, I'm going to ask you how did you feel, and what did you think when you heard that there was going to be a Poetry Group here? You can be quite honest.
Patricia: Yes, I will be. I'll be quite honest. If I were to put it in the nicest way, I'd say I was horrified! (Steph laughs) Because I'd been absolutely *no* good at all at poetry, ever in my whole life. I didn't comprehend it and I couldn't come to terms with it at all.
Steph: Right. Well, however did we persuade you to come to the group? I can't imagine, now.
Patricia: I think you simply invited me, and said 'Just try it,' and that's how it started.
Steph: And how long did you have to try it before you began to get interested?
Patricia: Oh, not long. I mean, you were a good poetry lady, excellent at it – so, no time at all. A couple or three goes and I was in and enjoying it. And it's been very . . . what's the word? . . . very educative for me. It's taught me a lot.
Steph: Can you say a bit more about that?
Patricia: Well, it's sometimes understanding what the poet meant. I used to find that very difficult. But you've explained very well what the poetry might mean, so now it has a quite different conception for me.
Steph: You used to use that word, didn't you? You used to say,

'Oh, it's far too *ARALDITE* for me!' (Patricia laughs.) And how is it for you now that we're constructing our own poetry?

Patricia: Exciting! Very exciting!

Steph: I know that one thing you've often said is that it makes you use your imagination.

Patricia: Yes. I just go into a different realm, a completely different world.

Steph: Do you see pictures in your head?

Patricia: Not so much. I think I'm a word person. So words pop up for me. I never thought I'd be in a poetry group, I was such a wild young thing, growing up. You don't expect, at nearly ninety, to start afresh with some literary work. But if we didn't have the group, it would be a big chunk out! I don't think there's anything else here that brings out the magic side of oneself.

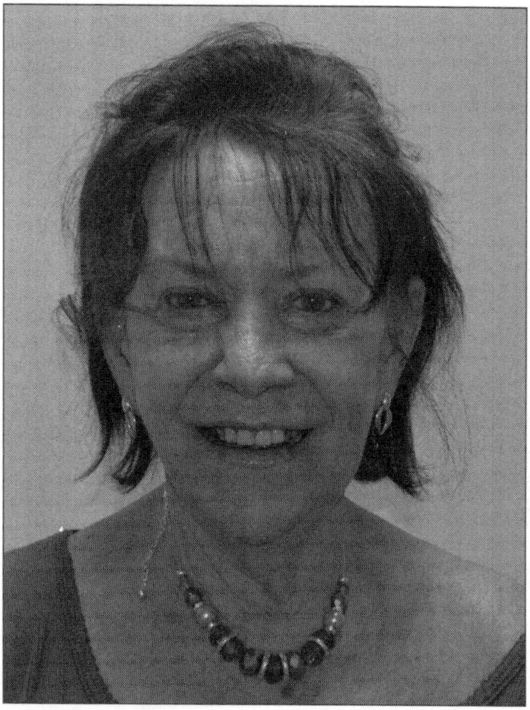

Interview – Fiona

Fiona: My name is Fiona McClean and I was born on 29th September 1946. So I'm the same age as you!
Steph: Tell me a bit about yourself, Fiona.
Fiona: Well, I'm Scottish, and proud of my roots. But I've travelled quite a lot in my life, first because of my parents, and afterwards, when I was married. I married a Frenchman I met in London. I was a radiographer then at St Ormond's Children's Hospital. I loved it.
Steph: How did you meet him?
Fiona: He used to come to see a friend, Ben, who lived in our house. I shared with four others. We all had a bedroom each, and shared the kitchen, bathroom and living room. I started my travelling then. He decided to buy a London taxi and five of us took it to France. There was François, who was driving, Ben, Steve, Zanie and me. We crossed the Pyrenees and we met another London taxi coming towards us!
Steph: How strange.
Fiona: And so we honked and waved madly. We went through Andorra, and the idea was to go to that town in Spain where they do the bull-running. That's when the bulls are let loose in the streets and all the men are chased by them. Sometimes

there are accidents. It was raining the night before and there wasn't enough room in the taxi for five people to sleep. One of the guys slept outside and got soaking wet. The next morning he got up and went to watch the bull-running. The rest of us slept right through it!

Steph: When did you get married?

Fiona: In Paris, after this trip. I liked living in Paris. We were in the 13th, an old district. We rented a big flat there, and I did my radiography in a very small village on the outskirts of Paris, Ivry-sur-Seine. I had to go on the Metro.

Steph: Did you already speak French when you got there?

Fiona: No, but I learned it all right, picked it up fast. And with my husband helping. François worked for an airline company, and next we were sent off to Africa, to Zaire. That was quite fun. Except you had to be careful about robbery. We were there for about two years and then we came back to France. Next my husband said we had the choice of either Saudi Arabia or Tahiti. And, of course, I said Tahiti!

Steph: And was it a good choice?

Fiona: Yes, because Saudi wasn't very good for women in those days. It's getting better now. So off we went. There are some wonderful beaches.

Steph: I'll bet. Was there any question in your marriage of children?

Fiona: I asked my husband if he wanted any, but he didn't.

Steph: How was that for you?

Fiona: I was OK, I didn't mind. We were having a nice life together. Then we had a terrible row and decided to separate for a year. I went back to Scotland, and then I went to London again to stay with my friend, Noreen, an Irish girl. I did my radiography for an agency and they sent me all over the place. It was fun. I must have been in my thirties then. In the end François and I got divorced. I stayed in Tahiti though. I was OK on my own. I had lots of friends, I got another job.

There were always a lot of parties. I remember one funny incident. I'd been with friends to a café to listen to some Senegalese drummers and a Tahitian drumming band. I'd had a bit to drink. Driving myself home I failed to see a 'No Entry' sign that was partly obscured by a tree. So there I was, driving the wrong way up a one-way street, when out jumped a policeman! He poked his head in through the window and said, 'You've been drinking. Whatever are you doing in this rough area? It's not safe. And you can't drive in that state! Move over'.

Then he told his colleague to follow us in the Jeep, climbed into my driving seat and started off towards my address. After a little while I said, 'Do you mind going into that garage? I've got my empty gas cylinder in the back'. And not only did he turn into the garage but, when we got to my house, he lugged the new cylinder into my kitchen and connected it all up again. Wasn't I lucky!

I didn't leave Tahiti until I decided to retire, when I was 60-something. So one of the Tahitian girls at the hospital helped me with the paper-work, I got my retirement and flew back to London. I did stop off to look at retirement places in France, but they were awfully cold and insipid. Back in England I thought of Wisma Mulia.

Steph: Which you knew because of your mother?

Fiona: That's right.

Steph: How many times had you visited her here?

Fiona: Quite a few times. She was in Flat 5. Every time I get prescriptions from the surgery they still always write 'Flat 5'. My mother was alive when I came here, but she wasn't well and had been moved to a nursing home near Pitcombe. My niece and I keep a storage place in Pitcombe now, and it's got all sorts of stuff of Mum's in it.

Steph: And you moved into Wisma. Has it worked out well for you?

Fiona: Oh, yes. I like my room. It's peaceful, and I've got the best bit of the garden. It's beautiful. And it's good to be a part of a community of people like this one. I have lots of friends here, especially Patricia. She's a great laugh.

Steph: And, of course, you were lucky enough to have found a great companion in Becky.

Fiona: Yes! – I love that cat.

Steph: You never considered becoming Subud?

Fiona: Yes, I did in the beginning. I'm still trying!

Steph: Do you remember when, a couple of years ago, I decided to set up the poetry group?

Fiona: A couple of years ago! Has it really been that long?

Steph: Yes. What did you think?

Fiona: I thought it was marvellous. My mother had loved poetry, but it was never something I'd particularly gone for. But it was something new at Wisma so I thought I'd come along.

Steph: What have you liked best about it?

Fiona: The ideas that come out, and all the people. They are very nice, interesting people, with all their memories. I liked the Japanese poems we worked on. I want to buy one of the books for myself, and one for my cousin. And I've enjoyed the interview; it was fun.

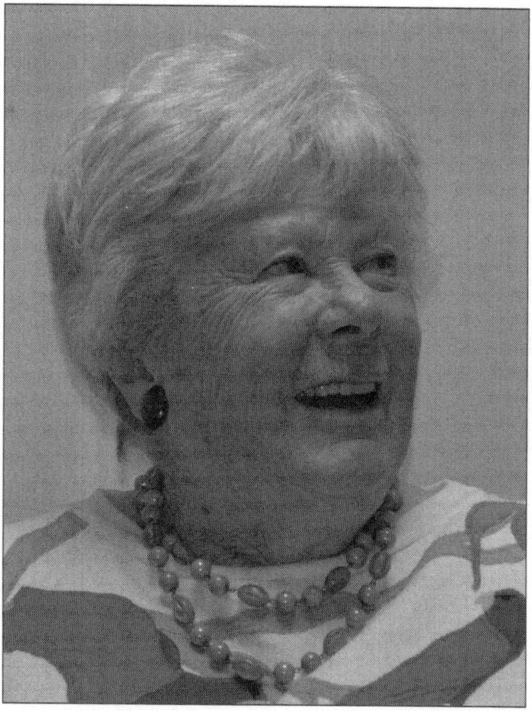

Interview – Maryse

Maryse: My name was Joan Margaret Phillips, from the French, 'Philippe'. Huguenot blood, you see. Now I'm Maryse Lawrie. I was born and brought up in Melbourne. But I'm very English now!
Steph: And what is your date of birth, Maryse?
Maryse: 1st November 1925. So I'm 85.
Steph: And can you tell me a bit about yourself?
Maryse: Well, I was always good at art. My mother wanted me to do housekeeping, or something like that. I said, 'No, I'm an artist,' and that was that. I knew as soon as I left school, what I was going to do. I started at Art College in Melbourne, where I specialised in Advertising Art.
Steph: And were you able to get work in that field?
Maryse: Australians love to travel, and after Art College I came to England. I came with three other girls. We went to Scotland, and had a lovely time going to dances. Then I went to an advertising agency in Bond Street. I designed ads for newspapers, and for *Vogue* – mainly fashion, make-up, jewellery.

Then I hitchhiked with another girl down to Italy. We went to Capri, and were having a great time there when my friend heard that her mother had died. She went home, and I took the bus back to Rome. There I got talking with a young man, and he asked me to marry him! He, poor chap, had to go back to North Africa.

Steph: Where did you meet the man who was to become your husband?

Maryse: In Australia. I'd had quite a few boyfriends and then I met a Scot who was travelling round the world on the ship he worked on. He had an MG which he kept on the ship, so we whizzed around the forests and the woods of Melbourne in that. It was great. He proposed to me on the phone, with an impatient man waiting outside to use the booth.

I came to England to wait for him to finish his tour. You came to England by ship in those days. It took 5 weeks. We came up through the Mediterranean. Finally we came up to Southampton. It was a lovely sunny May day and I could see them playing cricket on the green – I felt as if I could almost touch them, we were so close, it was lovely. In Australia in those days, one was very English orientated, so we knew all about it. In London I got on one of those tour buses and sat up on the top, and a woman came and sat opposite me. I looked at her and she was someone I knew in Melbourne! I was furious. (Steph laughs.)

At last I met up again with my husband. We couldn't decide which church we wanted to get married in, so we decided to have a civil marriage first. We got married at Caxton Hall in Knightsbridge or somewhere. In order to qualify for that I had to stay with somebody local. I had a friend, Mrs Doxford. She was very posh. She lived just round the corner from

Buckingham Palace. She had a son who was the 'Keeper of the Silver Stick'. (Steph and Maryse both laugh.) Maybe he walked round the Palace with his silver stick.

Steph: Looking fancy.

Maryse: Yes. I used to wake up in the morning in the early days there listening to the sound of the bells – Bow Bells was it? – and thinking, 'Wow, I'm in England, I'm really here!'

Steph: How was it that you became Subud?

Maryse: I was raised Church of England. My grandfather was a C. of E. Minister in Australia. My husband and I were looking for a good way of worshipping God, and we went to a place called Coombe Springs, down in Surrey I think it was. There was a Gurdjieff group there. We were doing Gurdjieff 'work' there when John Bennett* invited Bapak from Indonesia to speak to his pupils about Subud. So I was in at the beginning, when we all started in 1957. Rifai and I joined Subud together. He was opened* one day, and I was opened the next.

The marvellous thing about the latihan is that you don't need a priest. You can just sit quietly here, or anywhere and begin to feel the presence of the Almighty. We used to do latihan in what was called the Hut. There were not many places to do latihan at that time, so people used to come to Coombe Springs from all over the country. There was a book, and people signed in for their latihan time – thirty places per latihan, and you put your name down where you could. There were latihans from six at night to practically midnight. It was pretty wild there, with a lot of stuff people had to get rid of from their own and their

*John Bennett; *opened; see page 192.

families' pasts. It was a cleansing time. But that soon gave way to a much more relaxed and happy time.

Steph: That sounds very special. So, now you were together and members of Subud, how did your lives go along?

Maryse: We lived in London for a while. My husband was a Lecturer at London University. Then we moved to a dear little thatched cottage in Oxfordshire that looked out over the original White Horse.

Steph: That's you, looking out of that cottage window waiting for him to come home, isn't it? (indicating Maryse's painting.) You're a very talented artist.

Maryse: Thank you. Yes, I'm very fond of that painting. I loved that little cottage. But, you know, one really shouldn't go back. Years after I'd sold up I did go to look at it, and, do you know, the new people had taken off all the thatch and put on a tiled roof. I was quite shocked. It didn't look the same at all.

Steph: No, you're right, it doesn't always do to go back to places.

Maryse: When my husband died, I felt a bit vulnerable there on my own, all surrounded by fields. So I thought I'd come to the only Subud Residential Home in the world, here at Wisma Mulia. It's absolutely super. Rifai and I had never had children, which had left me free to travel about as a national helper, where you go round all the different groups and sit in on their goings-on and check out that everyone is happy, or if they need any questions answered, or anything tidying up in any way. So I knew so many Subud members. And I stayed with members while I was visiting too. Now so many of my Subud friends are here with me, aging most disgracefully! Very nice it is, very nice.

Steph: How did you react when you heard that there was going to be a Poetry Group here?

Maryse: I thought I'd go along and see what it was all about, but I wasn't into poetry particularly. My mother became what's called 'Dux' of the school, which meant top girl for something or other. She was given a huge book of Milton's 'Paradise Lost' with the most amazing illustrations by Gustave Doré.

Steph: The engraver?

Maryse: Do you know him?

Steph: Oh, yes. And my friend Trish once lent me his illustrated *The Rime of the Ancient Mariner* which was amazing, too.

Maryse: Really? This one was full of Angels and Devils all falling out of the sky. It was marvellous. I used to sit on the stairs and read that book . . . But, my dear, it's been a lovely experience here in the Poetry Group, really nice.

Steph: I'm glad. Which things have pleased you most?

Maryse: It opens up new vistas. In my normal life I don't think poetically, so it's been great. And I enjoyed it when we started making up poems together; that was funny! That one about St Augur was my favourite. And, of course, the 'Blue Bottle' poem. When I saw your blue bottle I was reminded of my French ancestor who came and settled in Bristol. I still feel most intrigued about my history and what my ancestor did with the blue glass that's become so famous.

Steph: Of course you do. You know that I often wear Bristol blue glass jewellery, don't I? Fancy your being a descendant of the man who began that!

Maryse: I've been to see where he lived.

Steph: Your Huguenot ancestor?

Maryse: Yes. He had a house in a very nice little square. And then he went up to Clifton and bought a house looking down on the estuary. He used to see all these sailing ships coming and going, so he thought, oh, I'd better have a go at that, so he sold his house and went off round the world. He decided to stay in Victoria.

Steph: What a good story. But, Maryse, I'll have to rein you in a bit, or we'll still be here at lunch time. Tell me, how do you feel on a Friday morning?

Maryse: It's all so pleasant here. Every day has its own excitements. Now . . . Friday morning – it's Poetry! Steph will be coming. She's always got lots of new ideas for us. I'm surprised she bothers to come to work with we old folk here . . . It's so sweet of you.

Steph: I wouldn't be without it. I'd miss it even more than you, maybe. Who knows?

Maryse: Well, the Group is certainly part of my life now, that's for sure. It adds to the interest of the place. Fridays would be very dull without you coming. I do like the old poems that you bring us, but also it's really fun to be creating a poem together in the group, and so interesting to hear just what each of us has to put into 'our' poem. Putting into verse what you think in a dull sort of way makes it more lyrical.

Steph: Do you think a poem has to have rhyme?

Maryse: I don't like it too rhymey, but it's nice to feel a rhythm.

Steph: And how do you feel about the fact that we're putting this book together?

Maryse: Aren't we clever! That's really exciting. I think it's amazing. It almost sounds unreal – but marvellous.

Steph: So, now you'll be recorded for posterity and you'll be an ancestor for somebody else.

Maryse: But they won't know which bits I've said.

Steph: Yes, they will, because I'll write that down. Anything else you'd like to say?

Maryse: Being an artist, colour is very important to me. I love it. If I hear colour named or suggested in a poem, that's really lovely. The poetry has been quite remarkable, really. It opens up aspects of ourselves we didn't know were there. It's broadening.

Steph: I think I remember you saying that once before. Didn't we put those words into 'What's In a Poem?'

Maryse: Oh, I don't remember, my dear.

Steph: Well, it's a good job I do, then. This has been a wonderful interview, Maryse. Thank you very much.

Maryse: It's been a pleasure.

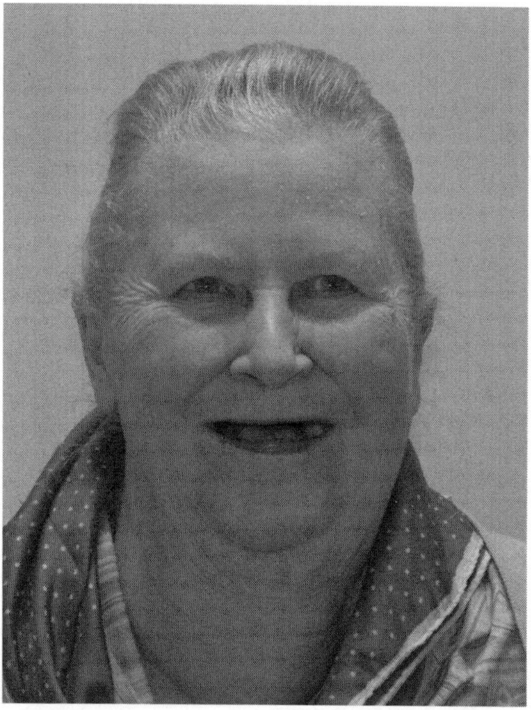

Interview – Nancy

Nancy: My name is Nancy Turner and I was born on 31st July 1935.
Steph: OK. So tell me a bit about yourself, Nancy.
Nancy: I was brought up in Arlingham on a farm, so I like animals. I miss the cows, the sound of them. The farmer here's got a few but he keeps them in during the winter.
Steph: Tell me about your family.
Nancy: I was the second youngest of four children. My father had been a farmer all his life. My grandparents lived in Frampton – their name was Betteridge. My grandfather had a pony and trap, so he used to take people to the station – me with him, if I wanted to go.

Children from the school would come and play at the farm – we'd climb on the hay. But we never went near the bull! We helped with the garden, two acres of it, as well. It was a mixed farm of about two hundred acres, with about sixty cows, and crops of wheat – oats, I suppose. My Mum always kept chickens, and had the egg money. My brother has the farm now.
Steph: What was the name of your farm?
Nancy: It was called Milton End Farm.
Steph: We've got a poem that's called 'Daybreak at Milton End Farm', which is all about you.

Nancy: Is there?

Steph: Yes. It's about you getting up in the morning to all the sounds of the farm.

Nancy: Oh yes, the cows 'n that.

Steph: It sounds like a nice life.

Nancy: Yes, it was. We went to school near Arlingham. There were good and bad teachers. Mrs Griffiths, she was Welsh. She used to get up school trips for us. One of the teachers used to cane the kids, I sometimes got caned. When I left school I stayed on the farm. My Dad gave me some hens – Rhode Island Reds. I had the money from the eggs. Hens are stupid birds! I had to be careful the foxes didn't get in. There was an old ruined house near our farm and the foxes used to breed in there. When I retired I went into a retirement home in Slimbridge, just by the Tudor Arms.

Steph: So what brought you here?

Nancy: The home was closed down and made into flats.

Steph: That must have been difficult for you.

Nancy: Yes, it was, because there were eight of us, and we all wanted to stop there.

Nancy: So you knew everyone really well, and now you were going to be split up?

Nancy: That's right. They all went to different places.

Steph: How did you choose Wisma?

Nancy: Mrs Hawkins chose it for me. She said she'd 'pulled some strings' to get me in. I moved in at apple time, so it must have been about October.

Steph: Do you know how long you've been here?

Nancy: About five years now.

Steph: And has it turned out OK?

Nancy: Yes, I like it. I like painting. I go to the art class here. And I like to make friends. I've made friends with Naomi. She hasn't been here very long.

Steph: Do you have any other special friends?

Nancy: Mmm. I like Julie. She's the Head Girl.

Steph: That's a good name for her. What did you think about a Poetry Group starting here?

Nancy: I do like poetry. I liked it at school. All children do, don't they? My daughter, when she was about five, that's all she wanted was a poetry book, because they were doing poetry at school. Anyway, Aine was interested, so I thought I'd come along and see what it was like.

Steph: And what did you think?

Nancy: I enjoyed it.

Steph: What was the best thing about it for you?

Nancy: When you recite the poems, I think. I like hearing them. I'm a good listener.

Steph: Yes, you are. I remember we did persuade you to give a little performance in last year's concert. You were a bit nervous, weren't you?

Nancy: Oh, yes! I performed, didn't I?

Steph: Yes. And what do you think about our book, with your contributions to the poems and this interview and your photograph in it?

Nancy: I think it's a really good idea. You're going to sell the book, aren't you? I didn't expect it.

Steph: And do you remember the title we all agreed on?

Nancy: No, what was it?

Steph: It's going to be *Songs From an Armchair: a book in praise of old age*.

Nancy: Oh, that's a good idea, 'cos we're all getting on a bit, aren't we?

Steph: Well, we are, and you're all a bit special, too. You're not your average elderly people, are you? You're all a bit lively, and single-minded, I find.

Nancy: (laughing) Suppose we are.

Steph: Well, thank you very much for your contribution this morning, Nancy.

Nancy: I've liked it.

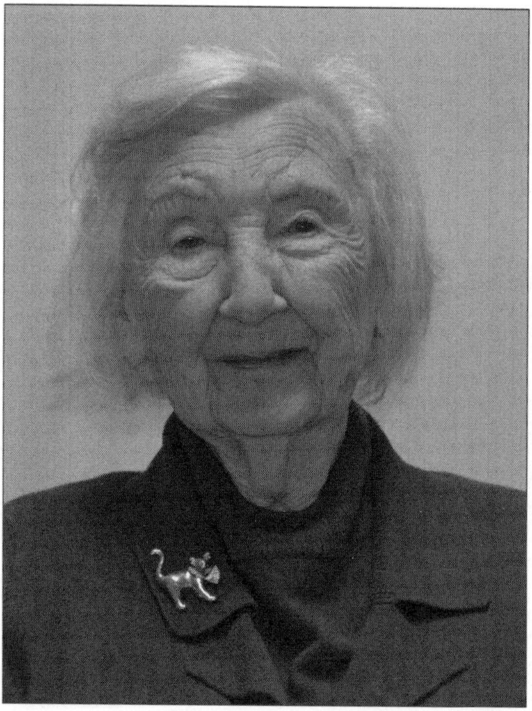

Interview – Naomi

Steph: Can you give me your name and date of birth first?
Naomi: Do you want them all?
Steph: Yes, please.
Naomi: Naomi Marguerite Constance Nicholls. When I married we were Jones at first, and then we adopted the other name and became McLauren-Jones because . . . Oh, I forget why.
Steph: Because Jones is ordinary?
Naomi: Yes!
Steph: Like me. I'm a Smith.
Naomi: (laughing) Well, 'Smith and Jones'.
Steph: Oh, yes! And what's your date of birth, Naomi?
Naomi: January the 18th 1918.
Steph: You look very good for 93! Can you tell me a little bit about yourself?
Naomi: What I've done in my life?
Steph: Mm. Anything at all of interest in your life. Did you have brothers and sisters, for example?
Naomi: Oh, I had a sister, but I never see her.
Steph: Were you brought up in the north of England?
Naomi: No. I was brought up in a village between Painswick and Gloucester, Upton St Leonards.

Steph: Lovely. Beautiful area.

Naomi: I suppose I didn't take much notice of it when I was little.

Steph: And what did your father do?

Naomi: He was a builder. He had two brothers. Oh, it's such a *long* time ago.

Steph: Don't worry. I only want to hear the bits it's easy for you to remember.

Naomi: Well, I went to Gloucester High School, and then to a Quaker Boarding School in Somerset.

Steph: You were a 'cradle' Quaker, then?

Naomi: Yes, 'birthright'.

Steph: Did you appreciate that spiritual part of your life?

Naomi: Not then, no.

Steph: It was just a way of being?

Naomi: Yes. You did what you did, and that was that.

Steph: Did you like being a boarder?

Naomi: Oh, I loved it.

Steph: When did you learn to play the piano?

Naomi: When I was five. I can't remember it. When I went away to school there was a nice man who taught me. Then, in 1936, I did a course of what was called 'Dalcroze Eurythmics' – music and movement.

Steph: Fabulous! I've never met anyone who actually did that!

Naomi: Oh, have you heard of it?

Steph: Yes.

Naomi: Good gracious. I'm astonished.

Steph: That may be because I was trained for the theatre, and I did a lot of reading around the subject. Tell me how it worked.

Naomi: Well, I don't know what happened to it, or if they do it any more. I was hoping to teach it, but then the war came. Ruined everything.
Steph: Did you find dancing easy? You're naturally very graceful.
Naomi: I think so – I just did it.
Steph: Are there any photos of you dancing?
Naomi: I don't know what's happened to them.
Steph: What a shame. That would have been lovely to show the grandchildren, you, drifting about like Isadora Duncan.
Naomi: Yes, she was about at the same sort of time. I never saw her dance, but I knew her name, of course.
Steph: She came to an untimely end.
Naomi: Did she? What happened to her?
Steph: I believe the story goes that she was driving in an open carriage, with a long and gauzy scarf wrapped round her neck. And one end of the scarf blew out of the carriage and got wound up in the wheel, and she was strangled.
Nancy: That's right! Now you mention it, I do remember hearing that.
Steph: And what did you do during the war?
Naomi: In the war . . . I was going back to my Eurythmics for another year. When the war came I scrapped that. After about a year, I went into the Land Army. Yes, best years of my life.
Steph: Really?
Naomi: Oh, yes. I just loved being outside. I didn't have anything to do with the animals, but I was the tractor driver! It was just coming in. That was near Gloucester. I lived at home and went to the farm every day. I was the only girl. In those

days nothing had started, really. You felt you were doing something useful.

Steph: When did you meet your husband?

Naomi: During the war. He also went to a Quaker school, up in the north. Down here he went to Gloucester Quaker Meeting. And he got a job with my father's firm.

Steph: Did he court you for a long time?

Naomi: I think so. That's how it went in those days. We had children: Felicity, Alistair, Hannah and Sarah. I always said I wouldn't have children!

Steph: You didn't do very well then, did you!

Naomi: Four children. It seems amazing.

Steph: Do you remember how long you've been at Wisma now?

Naomi: Last year I came.

Steph: Is it working out well for you?

Naomi: It's all right here, I like it. I'm very lucky with this flat. I have a kitchen and a bathroom. I don't cook now. I miss it, really – I loved cooking. But seeing that field there, with its ups and downs, and when he brings the tractor, it reminds me of when I used to plough.

Steph: Of course. Nice memories just outside your window. What made you come along to the Poetry Group?

Naomi: I don't know. Perhaps I saw it advertised and thought 'that would be interesting'.

Steph: And have you enjoyed it?

Naomi: Oh, yes! It hasn't finished, has it?

Steph: No. But we'll be having a break while I go to Thailand. That's when I'll be working on our book. But I'll be back in

April and we'll start again.

Naomi: Oh, that's good. It's something different. I liked poetry as a girl at school. As long as there's something going on. That's what I like. I'm very fortunate. I've done very well.

Steph: Last question. What do you think about the fact that the Poetry group is going to publish a book?

Naomi: Oh, I think it's extraordinary.

Steph: Well, Naomi, thank you for doing this lovely interview.

Naomi: Oh, my dear, it's my pleasure.

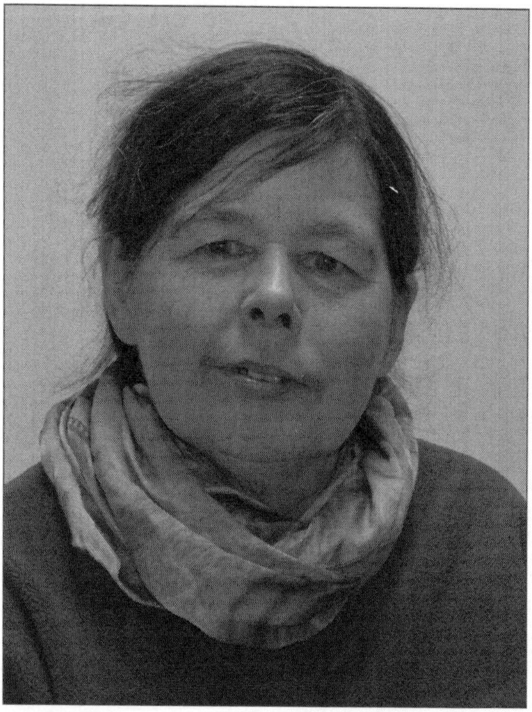

Interview – Monica

Steph: First, please can you give me your name and date of birth?
Monica: 30th January 1949. Monica Margaret Catherine Jones. I added the 'Monica' when I became a member of Subud.
Steph: It's going to be impossible, with the life you've led, to give a potted history. But could you have a stab at it?
Monica: Give you the highlights? Well, I grew up in Hertfordshire, widowed mother, one older sister. A very happy childhood on the whole, I think. My mother was quite a strong, demanding personality, and she was also very loving, so I think we felt a lot of security in our childhood. Health and safety wasn't an issue then, you know, so we spent a lot of time up the woods, lighting fires and generally running wild.

Then University was North Wales, Bangor, a very beautiful place with the mountains and the sea, and very different from home. I think, with coming from a very conservative area and a conservative family, it was quite a revelation to start reading George Orwell and the poets of the thirties – really opened my mind.
Steph: Can you tell me a little about your parents?
Monica: My father's first job was in the New Zealand Merchant

Navy. He was First Mate on the *Rangitata*, which was like a New Zealand Cunard Line. During the war they commandeered all these ships, and the *Rangitata* became a troop ship, going to and fro, taking troops from all over the Commonwealth to North Africa. He came to Britain, met my mum, and then, after they were married, he volunteered for the RAF. He wanted to train as a pilot but he ended up as a navigator for the bombers in Coastal Command. He was very fortunate to survive the war; only a third of his squadron did.

After the war he got a job at the Air Ministry. But he'd become addicted to flying, he loved it. He didn't want a desk job. So they found him a job in navigation. As my mother tells it, one day he landed at Gatwick, got out of the plane, staggered a few yards and collapsed, and died later in hospital. I think I was about six weeks old.

Steph: Terrible for your mum.

Monica: Exactly. I don't think she ever really got over it. She had been a secretary for the War Office in the Fire Department during the war. She had many interesting jobs when she was supporting the family. Once she applied for a job at the grammar school where I was, and was accepted as a school secretary. It was a little strange! She knew far too much about what the teachers said to one another, and she wasn't always tactful about repeating that!

I do remember, when we were in the lower part of the school, all the other kids were scared of her, and they'd say, will you come to the office with me to see your mum? (laughing) She tended to be rather irascible and she said just what came

into her head. But it scared people. She was very blunt, and she often embarrassed me. She was a character.
Steph: Do you think you've inherited anything of her?
Monica: Yes, I think her love of life. She enjoyed things, had an uproarious sense of humour. She was great fun, and warm-hearted and generous. She had a lot that was very good about her. She gave us courage, actually, she was such a battler. She'd say, 'Life is bloody tough, but you've got to get on with it'.
Steph: Was there a spiritual element to your upbringing?
Monica: There was, actually, because she went to this thing called The Gurdjieff Teaching. And that was very important in her life. I remember she used to leave us with the babysitter and go off on a Wednesday night, and it always struck me that she was very happy when she came back, and something in her had changed. Serenity and – more than that – a kind of uplifting. Once I said, 'Have you been to a party?' and she laughed. I remember that.
Steph: So, did you follow in her footsteps early, or later?
Monica: Well, we got taken to some of the weekend gatherings, and we'd be left with a couple of child-minders, and we might go into the woods, and maybe we made a nature table, I don't know what we did. We'd just be together, the kids of these Gurdjieff group members, and it was a nice atmosphere. But then Uncle Simon, who was Uncle John to me then, found Subud. I think he was in the second group that Bapak opened. He was immediately very changed by Subud. He tried to tell my mum about it and I think she understood that the latihan is a very powerful thing, and she was a bit scared of it because it involves letting go.

Steph: Absolutely. You're surrendering your will.
Monica: I think it was precisely that. She was very spiritual, but didn't want to let go of her will. She got very annoyed about little things, like name change, which is not obligatory – no-one has to take a new name.
Steph: What is the idea of it, though?
Monica: I think it expresses an understanding that your life has changed. Your whole sense of the world changes when you're opened.
Steph: So it's a marker?
Monica: It's a marker, yes. For some people. I think it's also a reminder of what needs to change in you. You get people, especially people who are very wise in Subud, you get them to test what your name should be . . . I hate to tell you that my name is said to mean 'Wisdom'. (laughs) I've made enough foolish blunders in my life, so it probably is a good marker.
Steph: When did you join Subud?
Monica: Oh, late, compared to some people here. Six years ago.
Steph: Oh, not long ago.
Monica: No. I took a long time. Partly because of my mother's hostility to it, I think; partly because, for a long time, many years, I was a materialist, and didn't accept that there could be anything beyond the physical body and the material world. You lead a reasonable life, you're good to your friends, you go into the ground and your body rots – and that's it. And then I got into Quakerism . . . I'll try to explain.

After University I went to Egypt. I did an MA and then went through the Voluntary Service Overseas and taught

English in the English Department of Alexandria University. So then I met my husband. We were both twenty-six. Eventually we got married. We lived with his mum for a long time, which wasn't easy. It was a huge, extended family and the house was very crowded.

Steph: And there was that massive cultural divide you had to contend with.

Monica: Yes, and I was always making mistakes and learning – a steep learning curve, being an Egyptian daughter-in-law! Then we went to the States, and I got my PhD from Purdue. I wrote about Californian novelists in the 1930s. Most of them were pretty obscure; John Steinbeck, obviously, and Upton Sinclair, you know, of *The Jungle* – he actually ran for Governor of California, and very nearly won. And then there was Aldous Huxley.

Steph: Was he a Californian?

Monica: He settled there. It was interesting to have a British author. And then, of course, there was Nathaniel West, *The Day of the Locust*; it's a kind of satire on Hollywood. And my husband wrote on Renaissance Theatre. He left Purdue and had a year at Johns Hopkins, and then he finished his PhD at the State University of New York at Stony Brook. It was a great place, we enjoyed that. I had various part-time teaching jobs. When we were in Baltimore while he was at Johns Hopkins, I had a very split existence. During the daytime I would teach at Goucher College, which was a sort of adjunct of Johns Hopkins – young ladies, very expensive, very posh. I'd have questions like, 'My father's the Cultural Attaché in Caracas, but I'm having my horse shipped to Baltimore. Do you know of any good livery stables?'

So this was the daytime teaching. And then, in the evening, I'd go to the Community College of Baltimore, where they were Chinese, Mexican, West African, Polish. Some of them didn't even have visas. I used to teach English as a second language.

Steph: Which did you prefer?

Monica: Oh, I think probably the evening class, actually. They were such fun! (laughing) And there were big debates about Communism. They were a priceless group.

Then my mother got ill. She'd had cancer for a long time, but now things were coming to a head. I came back to Britain. That's when I got the job at UWE, the University of the West of England. Things do sometimes just seem providential. There was an ad in the *Chronicle for Higher Education*, which is like the *Times Educational Supplement*, and it offered a position for an Americanist, in Bristol. And I applied and flew there at my own expense, with no idea of whether I'd get the job. I think there were four other applicants. I just, somehow, went with the flow. And, yes, I was offered the job, which meant that I was able to bring my mother to Bristol and look after her. And she died there at the flat in Bristol. She'd always said, 'I don't want to go into a home', she dreaded that. It was something I was able to do for her, not very competently, but as best I could. That made me happy. Once I said, 'Do you like living here, Mum?', and although I'd called her Mum, she said, 'Well, you're very kind and loving, whoever you are'.

And then I went on doing the job. I got very active, because my husband was back in Egypt then. So I got very involved in left wing politics. Then he came over for a bit, with his brand new PhD, and the idea was that he'd get work here. Well, he applied for eighty jobs.

Steph: Eighty? How did you explain that?

Monica: I think there was a lot of racism, and he was in his forties and had no publications. His long Egyptian name didn't help – he wanted to teach English Literature. In the States things were more multi-cultural; we had Indian friends who got jobs. But in Britain it was still more insular then. We still are. One of the most telling experiences was that he wrote for a job teaching literature, and he got back a package for teaching Computer Science. They saw the name and just assumed oh, he wants a science job.

Steph: That was a humiliating experience. How did he cope with it?

Monica: Well, very badly. He found it bitterly depressing, disappointing. He was on his own all day while I was teaching, and after several months he just said, 'Look, this isn't working out. I have to go back.' Shortly after that I resigned. I was fed up with all the bureaucratic procedures, not the teaching – pointless paper exercises that were just assisting some senior manager's promotion. I went to Egypt, and found I was in the reverse position to Essam. I could have had a teaching job, but I didn't want to go back to what I was doing before. So after 5 months we agreed that it wasn't working. We've always respected each other's space. So now we have a sort of

commuter marriage. He sometimes comes here, but it's easier if I go there. The cost of living is cheaper there.
Steph: And does it work well?
Monica: Yes, actually, it does. He's got a lot of space there. He worked very hard for a few years in the Lebanon and he bought two flats, one above the other like a maisonette. So I live on the top floor.

Back in Britain I had various jobs. I didn't want to get back into academe. I went a bit wild – which most people do when they're nineteen! Did some anti-nuclear protesting. Got nicked a few times. Did one major action with a very nice Quaker. Paul and I broke into RAF Fairford just before the Iraq war and damaged some vehicles that were going to carry the bombs onto the planes.

We stood trial twice for that, because the Jury couldn't agree the first time round. We appealed to what were then the Law Lords (that later became the Supreme Court). Of course, what we wanted to say was that the war was illegal, but the Law Lords ruled that out decisively. But it took years to get to that point. We were allowed to say that we honestly believed there would be war crimes. Anyway, it seemed a bit ironic, and I realised what a lottery the Jury is. I was given a curfew for six months – because I'd had previous convictions.
Steph: That must have been difficult.
Monica: Not really. I did a lot of baking! Funnily enough, I was allowed out for latihan twice a week. I'd said, 'I do have a religious observance in the evenings'. I was thinking, goodness, I hope I don't have to explain all about Subud in open court,

that could be quite difficult. But the judge didn't even ask what it was and said, 'Very well then, you may be relieved of your curfew on Thursdays and Saturdays'. He was very reasonable. He obviously saw me as a hopeless case.

Steph: Are you a risk-taker? Do you like danger?

Monica: I don't know. Someone said about me that I like to live life on the edge. I didn't think that about myself. But I think since I've been in Subud I've calmed down a lot, mellowed a bit. Before, I was a full-on adrenalin addict.

Steph: And what came next?

Monica: That would be Subud, I suppose. Interesting, really. I got involved with the Quakers, partly through the anti-war actions and peace campaigns. And because I was like my mum and said just what came into my head. I saw how they dealt with the police, for example. Where I'd say exactly what I thought, I saw that Quakers would be firm but polite. They knew just where to draw the line. This impressed me. And I could see something in their eyes. I kept thinking – because I was still a materialist – I kept thinking, they're tapping something. They know something. What is it they've got? I knew I hadn't got what I could see in their eyes. So I got curious.

I did about ten days for a minor thing, a non-payment of a fine. While I was in prison I had the chance to attend a Quaker meeting. Then, a few weeks later, when I wasn't in prison any more, I got a phone call from a Quaker saying, we know you're interested in Palestine. Would you like to come and do an appeal for any Palestine cause you're involved in? So I went along to their meeting, and I got such a good feeling from that that I kept on going back. It sort of drew me in. That's when, after years of Simon gently nudging me, and lending me books, I had a sort of feeling of what Subud could be. I still thought you could go to a latihan and just walk out, like at a Quaker meeting, saying, oh, that was interesting. The point about the latihan is, it's such a powerful experience, it's irreversible. Once you've been opened, you'll always be opened.

Steph: I think you once said to me, either you get opened or you don't.

Monica: Oh, no. That's not quite true. I suppose what I meant was, some people seem to have a block. That block can be dissolved over time. I know one woman – I think she's amazing – she went to latihan for nine years without consciously feeling anything.

Steph: Why did she keep going?

Monica: That's the interesting question. Sometimes Bapak would say to people who said 'I don't receive anything', 'Just keep doing the latihan'. Some people just go click, like that, you know?

Steph: Was it like that for you?

Monica: No. It took me about three weeks. Then it just took off, physically. I'll tell you some of it. I started to sway a bit, that was the first thing. It often seems to be like that: people feel as if they're being gently pushed.

And my friend Alex who's in Subud told me about one thing that Rabbis say, that prayer begins like a candle flame. You know how when Jewish people are praying you see them doing this (rocking back and forth)? He said that's like the candle flame, and that it's the beginning of the way to God. Bapak never claimed that the latihan was separate or distinct from other spiritual experiences. It's not a religion, that's very important. You could be Muslim, Jewish, Christian. You could be an agnostic.

Steph: What is it, if not a religion?

Monica: It's a receiving. The Quakers had it, they called it The Light. The early Quakers spoke in tongues, and they shook – that's why they were called Quakers. I know someone who told me that when he was opened, and he was opened by Bapak, Bapak just said, 'Begin', and his knees simply buckled, he fell to his knees, shaking. When Bapak went to the Exeter Meeting House he stood very quietly for a few minutes and then said: 'The latihan was here, three hundred years ago'.

So that's why I find it very easy to be a Quaker in Subud, because I think Quakerism today is just a diluted form of what the latihan was.

Steph: So if you're asked what your religion is, you say that you're a Quaker?

Monica: I say that I'm a Quaker, yes.

Steph: Are you now a Member?

Monica: Yes. When did I apply . . . ? Yes, 2005. Just after I was opened in Subud. Lots of people don't, but you are encouraged to have an orthodoxy. I think it's partly because Bapak didn't want people who lived, for example, in Muslim- or Catholic-based countries to make themselves look distinct or peculiar. He wanted them to blend in. So he said, if you go to church don't suddenly start doing a latihan, they'll think you're weird. Just say the prayers like everybody else, follow the practices of the orthodoxy. You will have something else that will enhance your spiritual practice.

Steph: What brought you to Wisma?

Monica: Simon, I think. Partly what became a very strong receiving that I should get out of Bristol. I used to come and visit Simon every few weeks. The trouble with coming from Bristol on public transport was that I'd get stuck here overnight. Simon is uncanny. He often knows what's going to happen before you do! One day he said, 'I'll just show you what they've been doing in the Cottage'.

So I followed him up, and of course I said, oh yes, that's nice. And he said, why don't you stay here overnight and see how you like it? I woke up in the morning and felt . . . well, almost irrationally happy. I mean, the sun was shining, the birds were singing. But it was more than that. There was an extra peace and happiness. And I thought of all the people who had been and are living here, and I thought, we're being gathered in. So that was the feeling.

I moved in about six weeks later. And Philip gave me the chance to test-drive the flat before I moved in. You don't often get that! It's very nice here. You've got a ready-made set of friends on your doorstep. The fact that people here are eighty and ninety means nothing.

Steph: No – I've found that out! Is the membership of Subud increasing or decreasing, do you think?

Monica: In the west it's decreasing, I think. And we do have a responsibility. Bapak was very clear, actually. He said to people, 'Do enterprises'. And he didn't mean, be Donald Trump, make lots of money. He meant, rather like the Quakers; they had chocolate factories, and did a great deal in the community. He meant in that kind of spirit. Or like in a Muslim community where, if someone comes into money, they say that God has 'opened the way'. Then they use the money to build a mosque or a clinic.

Steph: And is this happening in Subud?

Monica: Unfortunately, not here, really. More in other countries. In Indonesia there are children's homes, there's a school, there's a project for mine workers. I think in South America they have family education programmes, and things for nursing mothers. In Congo there's a children's home. There are a couple of projects in India. There is a Subud Charitable Association called Susila Dharma. The British branch raises most of the money, while Susila Dharma International seems to do most of the hands-on work with the projects.

Steph: So do you have ideas about how enterprise could be encouraged in Britain?

Monica: (laughs) I was going to ask you about this. You wrote a story which featured a charity shop. I wondered if that had been a part of your experiences.

Steph: No, never.

Monica: You invented it very imaginatively and very well. What we're talking about at the moment is a shop, and I'm looking at Stonehouse and Gloucester. I thought we'd do a pilot project for six months. If there aren't the people to keep it going, committing to a morning or an afternoon a week so it doesn't become too burdensome, if it doesn't work out we could say, well, we'll shut up shop now, but we made a few hundred quid.

We would hope to be a recycling project for the neighbourhood, and see where it went. There are three or four of us so far. We'll be looking for volunteers: maybe young people looking for some retail experience, or older people with time on their hands.

Steph: Well, maybe we'll find some of our readers come forward to offer help, you never know. Monica, thank you. It's been fascinating and a great pleasure, hearing about your life.

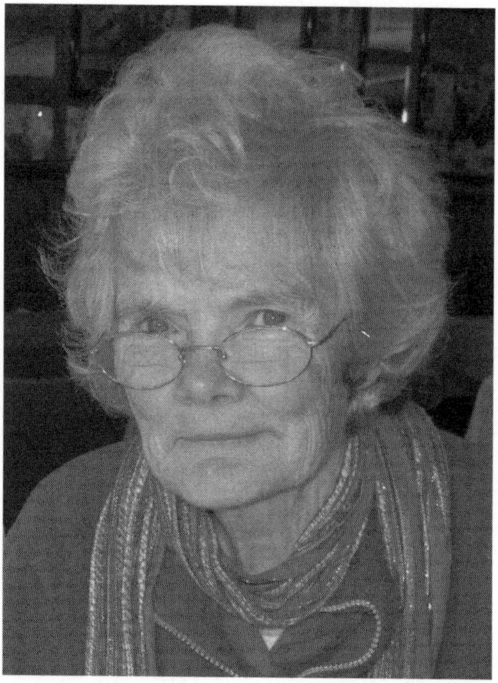

Interview – Hosanna

On the day that I was due to record my interview with Hosanna, she was too unwell for us to be able to go ahead.

During my three months in Thailand she made the decision to leave Wisma Mulia to live nearer to her daughter so, by the time I returned, she had left. In view of her struggles with ill-health we decided it would be best for me to ask a few questions of her over the telephone.

Hosanna is a very modest lady. As a late-comer to the group she was not sure she should be included at all. However, her gentle, spiritual poems add a special dimension to our book and we are delighted to have them, as well as her paintings of mandalas.

Here is a little about Hosanna's life:

Emily Hawkesworth was born on 20 October 1935.

At the age of 20 she answered an advertisement in *The Stage* magazine for an ASM (Assistant Stage Manager), was successful and began to work in repertory theatre, earning £3 per week. Later she also took small roles on stage. She met her husband, Leonard Kingston, a handsome leading man, and used to tour with him.

They had three children together. When the youngest was five years old, Emily did a special teacher's training designed for Mums who needed to fit their studies around school hours. She later took her B.Ed. in English at the college of the South Bank, and later still, her MA at Queen Mary's, London.

She worked in schools for a while, did some adult education, and finally settled in the role of one-to-one home tutor to children who had been excluded from school, or who were chronically ill and waiting to go to a special school. In those days she was lucky enough to be given a completely free rein about how she approached her pupils and decided what would be best for them to study.

She took the name Hosanna when she joined the Subud movement at Coombe Springs fifty-three years ago, after someone had lent her a book about it. Hosanna tells me that she is grateful for the strength and support of Subud. She feels it unites one and all, whether or not they practice a religion. All are included, which she comments is important today when there is so much violence, both associated with religion and in society at large. Subud succeeds in creating a community in which everyone is valued equally. She sees it as a very affirming thing, in a world where so many young people don't know they are valuable.

Asked for her thoughts about the Wisma Poetry Group she became positively animated. "I think it's a simply brilliant resource for Wisma Mulia," she said. "It was certainly a totally new experience for me, although I had come to poetry early myself, in my teens. TS Eliot's 'Four Quartets' was my big moment, I think! The group at Wisma offered the joy of poetry, plus the opportunity for anyone – including those who had never imagined they would be able to do such a thing – to contribute their own thoughts, words and feelings to a poem. It was so interesting to hear about people's lives. I learned a great deal about the members from hearing their various experiences. Yes, the Poetry Group will always remain one of my lovely memories of Wisma Mulia".

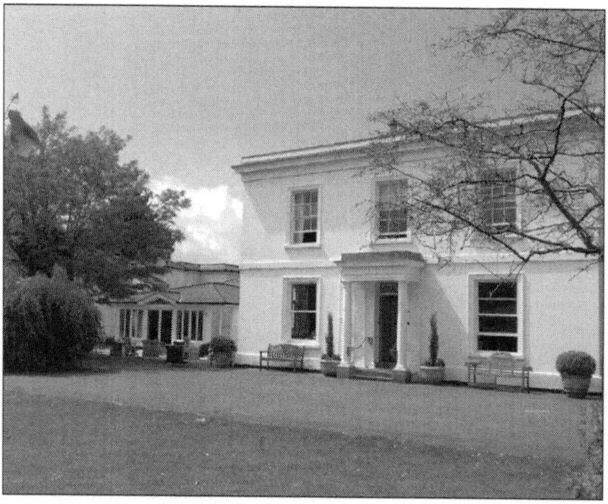

Chapter 8

About Wisma Mulia

'Plenty of love and lots of laughter.'
from the Wisma Mulia website

It was no surprise to me to hear a ten-year-old state his wish to 'retire early and come and live here'. The tranquil white building presides over beautiful, lovingly tended gardens in a prime position beside the Gloucester and Sharpness canal, a mile or two from the river Severn in the Cotswold village of Frampton-on-Severn.

It is known to the locals as 'the' place to live, and villagers are encouraged to get involved at Wisma. Some are employed there, others – often school and college students – volunteer there. Many attend the numerous events put on, from garden parties, barbecues and tea parties, to film evenings and concerts, getting to know the residents and returning again and again as friends.

Philip James and his committed team understand the need to ensure that life at Wisma is rich, comfortable and fulfilled. To quote Philip, 'The belief that every individual is valuable and deserves a rich and meaningful life inspires all we do at Wisma Mulia. At the heart of this is the desire to honour the residents' need to retain their own personality and sense of worth, whilst perhaps providing some care and support.'

Philip and the senior members of the staff team are not afraid to get their hands dirty, either. They have as much personal contact with the residents as do the amazing team of care staff, vivid in their fuchsia-coloured uniforms. Philip is as likely to be found under a chef's hat over the barbecue, in the stocks with a faceful of wet sponges at a garden party, or heaving a piece of furniture, as he is to be found behind his desk.

Jonsie, the activities organiser, is a marvel. In some miraculous way she manages to provide the residents with all the opportunities they would have in their own homes, from marmalade-making to helping prepare vegetables for lunch, from a visit to the pub for a meal, to a surprise performance from the local Silver Band. Nikki the hairdresser, Diana the Chiropodist, Cornelie the Art teacher, Simon the Keep-Fit instructor and, of course, Steph the Poetry lady, all put in their weekly appearances. Lyn is a willing driver and runner-of-errands for those who want to shop or be shopped for.

At 12.30 sharp every day, as many of the residents as are available congregate in the pretty dining-room for lunch. The tables for four are laid with silverware on coloured cotton tablecloths. Some of the residents confess that they have been putting on a few pounds since partaking regularly of the delicious meals prepared by Penny, Donna and their helpers. The sumptuous menus are printed out daily so that all can make their choice and are worthy of a professional restaurant.

But the barbecues are Philip's province. The community gathers at tables set in the shade of the acacia tree, and the wine and conversation flow in equal measure.

The over-riding philosophy at Wisma is that LIFE IS TO BE LIVED, and that is exactly what Wisma residents do, Subuds and non-Subuds alike. As lively and difficult to manage as a class of ten-year-olds, they have rendered my Friday mornings challenging, surprising, fascinating and enormously enjoyable.

Asterisked References *

A full explanation of these terms, and accounts of the lives of the referenced individuals, can be found at the Subud Great Britain official website:

http://www.subud.org.uk